The Palmström Syndrome

Dick de Mildt

The Palmström Syndrome

**Mass Murder and Motivation
A Study of Reluctance**

**Bibliographic Information published by the
Deutsche Nationalbibliothek**
The Deutsche Nationalbibliothek lists this publication in the Deutsche Nationalbibliografie; detailed bibliographic data is available online at http://dnb.d-nb.de.

Library of Congress Cataloging-in-Publication Data
A CIP catalog record for this book has been applied for at the Library of Congress.

The Palmström Syndrome is a revised edition of a book which appeared in 2018 in Dutch under the title *Straatgenoten* with Uitgeverij Verloren, Hilversum (ISBN 978-90-8704-711-5).

ISBN 978-3-631-80397-4 (Print)
E-ISBN 978-3-631-80772-9 (E-PDF)
E-ISBN 978-3-631-80773-6 (EPUB)
E-ISBN 978-3-631-80774-3 (MOBI)
DOI 10.3726/b16553

© Peter Lang GmbH
Internationaler Verlag der Wissenschaften
Berlin 2020
All rights reserved.

Peter Lang – Berlin · Bern · Bruxelles · New York · Oxford · Warszawa · Wien

All parts of this publication are protected by copyright. Any utilisation outside the strict limits of the copyright law, without the permission of the publisher, is forbidden and liable to prosecution. This applies in particular to reproductions, translations, microfilming, and storage and processing in electronic retrieval systems.

This publication has been peer reviewed.

www.peterlang.com

Dedicated to the memory of Lothar Kreyssig

Preface

> *What is man? Man is a two-legged animal of a specific bio-chemical composition. This composition determines all our physical and mental attributes. No man has attributes of himself; he can only have attributes of the species. You only have to determine that one member of the species can jump to know that all members can. Some will jump a little bit higher than others, but what is impossible to the species, is impossible to the individual. You do not need to examine every member of the human species to conclude that none of them can fly. And the individual has no property which not also belongs to the species.*
>
> M.S. Arnoni

The subject of this book originates in the stories of my father. They concerned his experiences as a young adult during the Second World War, both in his native country, The Netherlands, as well as in France, where he was captured on his route to Spain. He was imprisoned and finally sentenced to concentration camp detention for the duration of the war. While on a convicts' transport to Germany he had a miraculous escape and with some difficulty managed to find his way home, where he went into hiding. In many ways his stories were a lot like those in the books which boys of my generation devoured. They invariably pictured 'the good war' against the German occupiers as an exciting and patriotic adventure with a victorious ending. In this sense they also reflected much of the triumphant atmosphere of the annual commemorations and celebrations of my country's liberation from five years of German occupation. On the other hand, however, these same stories contained certain aspects which my youthful imagination found difficult or even outright impossible to understand. These 'mysterious' ingredients concerned the many violent deaths which occurred in them. They included relatives, French cell mates and other acquaintances of my father, who were killed by German hands. But whereas all of their stories were indeed shocking in themselves, not all were equally incomprehensible to me, however. There was, I felt, a significant 'qualitative' difference between them.

Both my father's mother and two of his cousins, for example, were killed by the Germans. Whereas his mother was gunned down in the street by a military patrol during an evening stroll, one of his cousins ended his life before a firing squad while the other perished in a concentration camp. The stories about their fate certainly made a deep impression on me, but somehow they still remained intelligible. The two cousins – brothers – died as a consequence of their resistance activities and from their letters I learned that they accepted their fate as the ultimate sacrifice of their principled rebellion against the regime of the German occupiers. And indeed, their sorry end seemed to retain a certain 'contextual logic'. After all, any resistance against a superior enemy carries the potential risk of severe punishment and the two brothers appear to have realized this. And whereas a similar logic was absent in the case of my grandmother, here it had been replaced by that of sheer coincidence. In an environment with very nervous and 'trigger-happy' German soldiers, just one day after the airborne operation of 17 September 1944 in the surroundings of Arnhem, she unfortunately found herself in the wrong place at the wrong time.

Tragic though their deaths were, conceptually they were still a far cry from those of the other victims present in my father's stories. These consisted of fellow inhabitants of his home town, who were taken away and murdered in faraway Poland for no other apparent reason than that they were considered 'life-unworthy', as they happened to be of Jewish ancestry. My father knew most of them from everyday life in pre-war times. They were middle-aged or even elderly men and women, local shopkeepers and others, whose families had worked and lived peacefully and inconspicuously within the community for generations and who constituted not even the remotest threat to the German war effort or the safety of the occupying troops. Their story seemed outright absurd to me.

As I came to learn more and more about their fate and that of millions like them in other parts of occupied Europe, this sense of absurdity obviously only increased. How was I to interpret what I 'witnessed' in their stories? Indeed, how was I to understand this enormous criminal drama which had taken place only shortly before I was born, amidst a cultural environment in which the generations of my parents and grandparents had lived and which I recognized as essentially mine as well? With the expansion of my knowledge of Hitler's genocidal universe, my preoccupation with these matters converted itself into something of a personal existential question. For if the actors of this universe belonged to the species of which I was a specimen, what then did that tell me about the characteristics of this species, and, by implication, about myself?

Prompted by my curiosity about the answers to these questions, I became a voracious reader on the subject and at the close of my history studies at the University of Leiden, around the mid-nineteen eighties, I had 'digested' a great many of them. What repeatedly struck me in the books I read, however, was the relative absence of interest in an objective, analytical approach to the background of the criminals involved. Whereas most authors described their unimaginable atrocities in considerable detail, hardly any of them made a serious effort to address their profile in a systematic and analytically objective fashion. This seemed all the more surprising to me as, ever since 1945, scores of criminal trials had been conducted against those responsible for these atrocities. Thus, I assumed that much information on their personal background and criminal development should be readily available in the documentation of these trials. For my doctoral thesis I therefore decided to study the defendants of the so-called Nuremberg 'Einsatzgruppen Trial', dubbed 'the biggest murder trial in history' by its chief prosecutor.[1] But whereas the published documentation of this trial again contained much on their crimes, it included disappointingly little on their personal histories.

Shortly after starting my work on this Nuremberg material in the Royal Library in The Hague, I stumbled upon a set of volumes entitled *Justiz und NS-Verbrechen* ['Justice and Nazi Crimes']. As I browsed through their contents I found that they contained hundreds of post-war trial judgments by West German courts on a dazzling variety of Nazi crimes, including a number of Einsatzgruppen cases. Different from the American documentation, however, these German trial judgments often contained substantial biographical information on the defendants. As it enabled me to study their personal profiles, including their 'route to crime', this material was precisely what I was looking for. While I acquainted myself with the idiosyncrasies of German criminal law and its application to the prosecution of Nazi criminals, I discovered that its focus on the subjective aspects pertaining to the defendants and their past behavior, formed a core ingredient of the German criminal law system. Coupled with the courts' relatively extensive motivation of their considerations and decisions, this turned these judgments into a unique and valuable source for the investigation of the perpetrators' profiles. Thus, I gratefully included the German Einsatzgruppen cases in my original research project.

Much to my surprise, the 'Justiz und NS-Verbrechen' collection of German trial judgments turned out not to be published in Germany, as one would have expected, but in my native country, The Netherlands. At the University of Amsterdam a Dutch professor of criminal law, named Frits Rüter, was in charge of the publication project. While working on his dissertation in Freiburg, Germany, way back in the nineteen sixties, Rüter had started to systematically collect the post-war German trial judgments against Nazi criminals. From 1968 onwards, he began to publish them in a series of hefty volumes.[2] After my graduation I contacted him with plans for further study and he was kind enough to offer me a PhD position at his institute. Thus, I spent the following years investigating the German trials and finally wrote my dissertation on a number of them. After completing my studies I joined Rüter as editor of the series.

While working on the JuNSV edition, I was again puzzled by the fact that so little use had been made of this judicial documentation for the investigation of the criminal actors involved in Hitler's murder programs.[3] On the whole, it appeared to me that many avoided the subject for some reason or other. And I came to wonder whether one of these reasons might not perhaps consist of the fact that this judicial documentation offered a somewhat unsettling perspective on the perpetrators' profiles; a perspective namely, that, instead of presenting them as one-dimensional incarnations of evil, showed them as identifiable representatives of the species. For those who consider these criminals sufficiently judged by their actions and who therefore reject any special interest in their backgrounds, such a perspective might indeed be reprehensible. Illustrative of such a view is perhaps the comment of the (once) renowned psychoanalyst, Bruno Bettelheim, on an effort to interpret the personalities of Nazi doctors: 'there are acts so vile that our task is to reject and prevent them, not to try to understand them....'[4] Considering Bettelheim's profession as well as his own thoughts on related subjects, this seems to me a curious point of view, but it is, no doubt, shared by many others.[5] Even though I can sympathize with the emotions behind such a position, however, for reasons set out in this book I cannot agree with it.

As said, the book's inspiration stems from my father's stories. But there is certainly also another inspirer of at least equal importance. This is the Auschwitz survivor whose observations stand above this introduction. It is with these observations in mind that this study was undertaken.[6]

Contents

I **The veiled image**	15
1. Little lumps of reality	15
2. The equilibrium of madness	20
3. The Laocoön in Nuremberg	27
4. The carrousel of fate	31
5. The opportunist route to crime (and back)	40
6. 'Show me yourself with your dog, and I'll tell you what you are'	51
II **Pars pro toto: Franz Stangl**	57
1. Conversations with the executioner	57
2. 'The Lord God knows me'	59
3. The dynamics of evil	61
The Austrian prologue	61
Hartheim and beyond	67
4. Truth and fiction	70
Duress of orders	72
The incorruptible policeman: Stangl's self-portrait	78
The awareness of injustice	81
III **The Palmström Syndrome**	87
1. A magical encounter	87
2. The criminal of the century	90
3. 'That which must not, cannot be' (I)	98
4. 'That which must not, cannot be' (II)	104
5. Facing 'impossible' facts	108

Postscript: the measure of all things 111

Appendix 115

Notes 131

Bibliography 147

Index on persons 163

I The veiled image

'Behind, be what there may,
I dare the hazard—I will lift the veil.'

Friedrich Schiller, *Das verschleierte Bild zu Saïs* (1795)
[*The Veiled Image at Sais*, translated by J. Merivale]

1 Little lumps of reality

Distance in space and time degrades intensity of awareness. So does magnitude. Seventeen is a figure which I know intimately like a friend; fifty billion is just a sound. A dog run over by a car upsets our emotional balance and digestion; three million Jews killed in Poland cause but a moderate uneasiness. Statistics don't bleed; it is the detail which counts. We are unable to embrace the total process with our awareness; we can only focus on little lumps of reality.

Arthur Koestler, 'On disbelieving atrocities', January 1944

Tarnopol, 7 April 1943
My beloved!

Before I leave this world, I want to leave behind a few lines to you, my loved ones. When this letter will reach you one day, I myself will no longer be there, nor will any of us. Our end is drawing near. One feels it, one knows it. Just like the innocent, defenseless Jews already executed, we are all condemned to death. In the very near future it will be our turn, as the small remainder left over from the mass murders. There is no way for us to escape this horrible, ghastly death.

At the very beginning (in June 1941) some 5000 men were killed, among them my husband. After six weeks, following a five-day search between the corpses, I found his body…. Since that day life has ceased for me. Not even in my girlish dreams could I once have wished for a better and more faithful companion. I was only granted two years and two months of happiness. And now? Tired from so much searching among the bodies, one was 'glad' to have found his as well; are there words in which to express these torments? (…)

Tarnopol, 26 April 1943

I am still alive and I want to describe to you what happened from the 7th to this day. Now then, it is told that everyone's turn comes up next. Galicia should be totally rid of Jews. Above all, the ghetto is to be eliminated by May 1. During the final days thousands have again been shot. Meeting-point was in our camp. Here the human victims were selected. In Petrikow it looks like this: before the grave one is stripped naked, then forced to kneel down and wait for the shot. The victims stand in line and await their turn. Moreover, they have to sort the first, the executed, in the graves so that the space is used well and order prevails. The entire procedure does not take long. In half an hour the clothes of the executed return to the camp. After the actions the Jewish council received a bill for 30,000 Zloty to pay for used bullets....

Why can we not cry, why can we not defend ourselves? How can one see so much innocent blood flowing and say nothing, do nothing and await the same death oneself? We are compelled to go under so miserably, so pitilessly.... Do you think we want to end this way, die this way? No! No! Despite all these experiences. The urge for self-preservation has now often become greater, the will to live stronger, the closer death is. It is beyond comprehension. (...)[1]

The farewell letters quoted here never reached their destination. More precisely, they were not even sent off to start with. We have no idea who wrote them, nor for whom they were intended. They were discovered only by chance among a pile of clothes belonging to the victims of an SS-extermination operation against the final inhabitants of the Tarnopol ghetto in the Ukraine, in May 1943. From their contents we can make out little more than that the female writer belonged to the small remainder of Galician Jews, who, only shortly before, had formed a population of some five-hundred thousand. Less than twenty-four months after the German invasion of the Soviet Union this population had vanished. It had been gassed in the extermination camps, shot inside and around the Galician towns and villages, or starved and worked to a miserable death in the numerous ghettos and forced labor camps spread across the area.

The Tarnopol letters form one of the 'little lumps of reality' which made up the colossal tragedy of the Nazi genocide. The few surviving lines of an anonymous victim allow us a fleeting glimpse of the unfathomable despair that echoed millionfold throughout the murderous universe that Europe had become during the years 1939 to 1945. These six years comprise the history of the mass extinction of millions of men, women and children, of all ages and nationalities, coming from all strata of society and from every town and village within occupied Europe. Within a brief span of time and with breath-taking ease, they were deprived of their civil rights, robbed of their possessions and physically annihilated. In the end, little more was left of their one-time existence than the birth certificates in the registers of their places of origins. And for some, even this barest testimonial of life was lacking. Thus, on 1 July, 1943, six baby boys born in the 'Gypsy camp' of Birkenau were formally registered as 'Z-8266' to 'Z-8271'. They would not live to see the end of the year. Like millions of others, they literally went up in smoke.[2]

From the outset, the absurd nature of Hitler's genocide frustrated the efforts to grasp its true meaning. Above all, this applied to the pauperized and starving populations of the Eastern European ghettos, who were forced to witness their approaching doom. For many the spectacle was too much to cope with and so they desperately sought to deny its inevitability. The Polish-Jewish educator Chaim Kaplan observed such efforts of his fellow Jews in the Warsaw ghetto and noted in his diary:

> The lack of reason for these murders especially troubles the inhabitants of the ghetto. In order to comfort ourselves we feel compelled to find some sort of system to explain these night-time murders. Everyone, afraid for his own skin, thinks to himself: If there is a system, every murder must have a cause; if there is a cause, nothing will happen to me since I am absolutely guiltless. [...]
>
> Tremendous intellectual effort is expended to find some motive behind all the slaughter. If there is a motive, there is a possibility of estimating the proximity of individual danger. But none of the theories have a leg to stand on; there are always incidents that do not fit the alleged motive, that are beyond calculation and unbounded by logic.[3]

And Kaplan also noted that the few who dared to publicly emphasize the latter were met with considerable animosity, as 'People do not want to die without cause.'[4]

That the ghetto inhabitants failed to discover this cause is hardly surprising. Eye to eye with persecutors who appeared to act at total random and completely isolated from the outside world, they lacked the wider perspective required for even a modest beginning of such an understanding. But even for contemporaries with a more comprehensive outlook, the reality remained hard enough to grasp. Thus, German-Jewish philosopher Hannah Arendt, who received reports on the mass extermination as late as 1943 in her American exile, initially refused to believe them as they seemed so utterly devoid of any power-political or military logic. And the leaders of the American Jewish Joint Distribution Committee and of other Jewish organizations outside occupied Europe reacted not all that differently.[5] And again, those who knew better and decided not to keep silent were met with disbelief and rejection. Typical in this respect were the experiences of the British-Hungarian writer Arthur Koestler in his efforts to inform public opinion on the ongoing massacres at the European continent. In 1943 the literary magazine *Horizon* published a chapter on the deportations from Koestler's new novel *Arrival and Departure*. Among the reactions he received were several highly negative ones, accusing the author of spreading horror stories to satisfy a morbid fantasy. On a more civilized tone, fellow writer and art expert Sir Osbert Sitwell inquired after the factual basis of Koestler's story. It prompted a furious reaction:

> Dear Sir
>
> In your letter you asked me the idiotic question whether the events described in *The Mixed Transport* were 'based on fact' or 'artistic fiction'.
>
> Had I published a chapter on Proust and mentioned his homosexuality, you would never have dared to ask a similar question, because you consider it your duty 'to know' although the evidence of this particular knowledge is less easily accessible than that of the massacre of three million humans. You would blush if you were found out not to have heard the name of any second-rate contemporary writer, painter or composer; you would blush if found out having ascribed a play by Sophocles to Euripides; but you don't blush and you have the brazenness to ask whether it is true that you are the contemporary of the greatest massacre in recorded history.
>
> If you tell me that you don't read newspapers, White Books, documentary pamphlets obtainable at W.H. Smith bookstalls – why on earth do you read *Horizon* and call yourself a member of the intelligentsia? I can't even say that I am sorry to be so rude. There is no excuse for you – for it is your duty to know and to be haunted by your knowledge. As long as you don't feel, against reason and independently of reason, ashamed to be alive while others are put to death; not guilty, sick humiliated because you were spared, you will remain what you are, an accomplice by omission.
>
> Yours truly,
> A.K.[6]

Koestler's bitterness resulted from the news that members of his family were among the murdered, but its deeper background consisted of his utter despair over the impenetrability of public opinion. In January 1944 he voiced this despair once again in an article in the New York Times, entitled 'On Disbelieving Atrocities':

> We, the screamers, have been at it now for about ten years. We started on the night when the epileptic van der Lubbe set fire to the German parliament; we said that if you don't quench those flames at once, they will spread all over the world; you thought we were maniacs. At present we have the mania of trying to tell you about the killing, by hot steam, mass-electrocution and live burial, of the total Jewish population of Europe. So far three million have died. It is the greatest mass-killing in recorded history; and it goes on daily, hourly, as regularly as the ticking of your watch. I have photographs before me on my desk while I am writing this, and that accounts for my emotion and bitterness. People died to smuggle them out of Poland; they thought it was worthwhile. The facts have been published in pamphlets, White Books, newspapers, magazines and what not. But the other day I met one of the best-known American journalists over here. He told me that in the course of some recent public opinion survey nine out of ten average American citizens, when asked whether they believed that the Nazis commit atrocities, answered that it was all propaganda lies, and that they didn't believe a word of it. … And meanwhile the watch goes on ticking. What can the screamers do but go on screaming, until they get blue in the face?[7]

In retrospect, the desperation of Koestler and his fellow screamers is all too understandable, of course. And we tend to blame their contemporaries for their persistent ignorance and lethargy in view of the ongoing horrors. But in all fairness it should perhaps be said that, instead of discrediting them, their disbelief to some extent speaks in their favor. For the reality of Hitler's gas chambers and mass graves was simply still unimaginable to most. The Nazi mass extermination policies were after all a highly revolutionary and unprecedented form of state-organized criminality, which, to all but the perpetrators themselves, must have appeared outright absurd. It was yet another Warsaw ghetto chronicler, Abraham Lewin, who realized this only too well:

> The level of Nazi brutality quite simply lies beyond our power to comprehend. It is inconceivable to us and will seem quite incredible to future generations, the product of our imagination, over-excited by misery and danger.[8]

What holds true for Lewin's 'future generations' certainly applied no less to contemporaries such as Sir Sitwell and his fellow skeptics. One could say that they were largely immune for the message as they were still *too decent* to grasp its implications. The post-war revelations of the Nuremberg trials certainly dealt a tremendous blow to this naivety, but they did not really solve the enigma of Hitler's genocide. On the contrary, if anything, they only increased its incomprehensibility.

2 The equilibrium of madness

Nowhere was the absurd nature of Hitler's genocide so vividly and penetratingly present as in the post-war courtrooms where his former associates and accomplices stood trial. They were the ones who had made the effort to turn their Führer's dystopia into reality, and so they were also the ones of whom it could be expected to solve the riddle. But their answers were outright mind-boggling, however. Take, for example, the ones from the former camp commander of Auschwitz, Rudolf Höss. Acting as a witness before the International Military Tribunal in Nuremberg, Höss informed the judges about his three-and-a-half year stay at the extermination camp:

> I commanded Auschwitz until 1 December 1943, and estimate that at least 2,500,000 victims were executed and exterminated there by gassing and burning, and at least another half million succumbed to starvation and disease making a total dead of about 3,000,000. This figure represents about 70 or 80 percent of all persons sent to Auschwitz as prisoners, the remainder having been selected and used for slave labour in the concentration camp industries; included among the executed and burned were approximately 20,000 Russian prisoners of war (previously screened out of prisoner-of-war cages by the Gestapo), who were delivered at Auschwitz in Wehrmacht transports operated by regular Wehrmacht officers and men. The remainder of the total number of victims included about 100,000 German Jews, and great numbers of citizens, mostly Jewish, from Holland, France, Belgium, Poland, Hungary, Czechoslovakia, Greece, or other counties. We executed about 400,000 Hungarian Jews alone at Auschwitz in the summer of 1944.[9]

In front of the same judges, Dieter Wisliceny – subordinate and former friend of deportation expert Adolf Eichmann – recalled the words with which his chief had taken his leave in February 1945: 'He said he would leap laughing into the grave because the feeling that he had 5 million people on his conscience would be for him a source of extraordinary satisfaction.'[10]

Hardly surprising, testimonies such as these turned Hitler's mass murder accomplices into objects of exasperated fascination in the eyes of post-war observers. Indeed, as one of them, Canadian historian Michael Marrus, aptly put it: 'For historians of the Holocaust, the greatest challenge has not been making sense of Hitler, but rather understanding why so many followed him down his murderous path.'[11] Among the earliest answers to this question was one, not by a historian but by an SS General, named Erich von dem Bach-Zelewski. Asked about the reasons behind all the slaughter, Bach, witness for the defense at the IMT trial, answered: 'If for years, for decades, a doctrine is preached to the effect that the Slav race is an inferior race, that the Jews are not even human beings, then an explosion of this sort is inevitable.'[12] And there could be no doubt about Bach's expertise in the matter, for as Heinrich Himmler's chief mass exterminator in the East he had personally orchestrated the outburst.[13]

Echoed by the Nuremberg judges in their verdict against the Third Reich's leaders, Bach's interpretation of Germany's recent genocidal past became the paradigm for the conventional perspective on Hitler's executioners. According to its line of reasoning, there existed a straight-forward causality between Nazi racial theories on the one hand, and its racial practices on the other. Thus, as Von dem Bach suggested, the barrage of ideological propaganda of the 1930s constituted a brainwashing of the German people to the extent that many of them willingly engaged in the subsequent mass murders. Viewed from this perspective, the gas chambers and mass graves of the Third Reich were the inevitable result of ideas disseminated by its racial hate propagandists among a particularly receptive audience.

An early example of such an interpretation can be found in the study of Dutch Auschwitz-survivor Elie A. Cohen. In March 1952, Cohen earned his M.D. with a dissertation on medical and psychological aspects of the German concentration camp. His study also appeared as a commercial edition and – unexpectedly – sold out in only a few days' time. It went through several reprints and was translated into English shortly after its first appearance.[14] In his book, Cohen addressed the murderous mind-set of the SS in psycho-analytical terms:

> The Super-ego, which as we know forms the introjection of the voice of the parents, the teachers and society, received a criminal contents with the SS men. From 1933 onwards, the Super-ego learned from society (radio, film, newspaper, book), from the teachers, and in many cases also from the parents: 'The Jews are our misfortune', 'the Jews must be wiped out', 'the Russians and Poles are inferior people, and so on. In this way, the SS men received a criminal Super-ego.... (...)
>
> Above all, it was the Super-ego which made it possible for the SS to kill Jews, Poles, Russians, and so on. One could even say: For the SS it was a necessity, for

according to Nazi ideology, these people were harmful elements. *To the SS their destruction was as necessary as the extermination of the Colorado-beetle in the Netherlands.*[15]

In her widely acclaimed book *The War against the Jews*, published nearly twenty-five years later, American historian Lucy Dawidowicz went a considerable step further as she explained the causes of this war by way of the collective insanity of the entire German people:

> Germans, otherwise individually rational, yielded themselves to pathological fantasies about the Jews. In that climate, where masses of Germans had lost the ability to distinguish between the real Jew and the mythic Jew of anti-Semitic invention, the chiliastic system of National Socialist beliefs could further influence their already distorted sense of reality. Belief in National Socialism was like belief in magic and witchcraft during the Middle Ages, similarly ruling and inflaming the minds of men. [...]
>
> In medieval days entire communities were seized with witchcraft hysteria, and in modern Germany the mass psychosis of anti-Semitism deranged a whole people. According to their system of beliefs, elimination of the Jews resembled medieval exorcism of the Devil. The accomplishment of both, it was variously held, would restore grace to the world.

As a result of this mass hysteria, the Germans considered themselves as

> latter-day Laocoöns in the grip of a death struggle. In a paranoid vision they believed themselves to be innocent and aggrieved victims, outwitted by the machinations of a super-cunning and all-powerful antagonist, engaged in a struggle for their very existence. [...] Consequently, in the deluded German mind, every Jewish man, woman, and child became a panoplied warrior of a vast Satanic fighting machine.[16]

And again twenty-five years later, another American bestselling author, political scientist Daniel Goldhagen, held out the very same message to his readers. In an extended echo of Dawidowicz, Goldhagen insisted that the explanation of the Nazi persecution of the Jews indeed lay in the delusional German obsession with the idea 'that Jewry was locked in an apocalyptic battle with Germandom.' Thus, as to Dawidowicz, to Goldhagen the Germans considered the extermination of the Jews necessary and justified: 'Letting such a mortal threat persist, fester, and build was to let down one's countrymen, to betray one's loved ones.'[17]

What interpretations such as those of Von dem Bach, Cohen, Dawidowicz and Goldhagen obviously have in common is their emphasis on the ideological, and even pathological motivation of the persecutors. Their behavior is considered to have been the outcome of a perverted world-view, an extreme and compulsive form of 'idealism', which considered the Jews as a mortal threat to their existence; a threat which dictated (and justified) their annihilation.

The continued popularity of such 'patho-ideological' Holocaust explanations is undoubtedly caused by their logical simplicity. For it is indeed clear that Hitler's terror and annihilation policies were ideologically inspired. Consequently, it also seems obvious to assume that their organizers and executors were motivated by the very same incentive. Moreover, such a conclusion appears to correspond with a rather basic view on the human condition and its psychology of motivation. Thus, we generally tend to relate extraordinary acts to correspondingly extraordinary motives. As every good deed is supposed to result from benevolent intentions, much the same applies to its opposite: bad deeds are commonly held to be caused by malignant intent. The 'logic of evil', therefore, requires that behind an extraordinary crime correspondingly exceptional evil motives lie hidden. Consequently, in the case of the extraordinary crime of the Nazi genocide there exists a strong inclination to rationalize the systematic physical extermination of millions of innocent and defenseless men, women and children by reference to the perpetrators' paranoid delirium. In this way one arrives at what might be dubbed the 'equilibrium of madness', by applying the circular formula that insanity breeds insanity. Essentially, this way of clarifying the incomprehensible by means of the incomprehensible is what characterizes the patho-ideological perspective on the perpetrators of Nazi genocide.

In spite of its apparent appeal, however, this 'Laoconian-style' interpretation does not answer the question posed by Michael Marrus in any satisfactory way. Indeed, among its flaws is its very simplicity. For if the crimes and criminals of Nazism could so easily be understood by reference to its pathological ideology, the question arises why so few of their contemporaries failed to grasp the logic at the time. If, as suggested in Laoconian-type retrospection, the blueprint of mass destruction was so unambiguously present in the propaganda speeches and writings of Adolf Hitler and his likes, and if the bloodlust flickered so prominently in the eyes of their followers, how ignorant must these contemporaries then not have been to overlook the message? For obvious reasons, an explicit answer to this question is generally avoided, but it is not all too difficult to figure out that it would not be particularly flattering for the victims of Nazi persecution.

That the patho-ideological perspectives lean heavily on hindsight simplifications also becomes clear if one takes a closer look at their core arguments. In order to disclose the psychology of the Third Reich mass murderer, its advocates recruit these arguments from leading Nazi hate propagandists and simply project them – quite often literally – onto the minds of the Nazi executioners.[18] But whoever considers Hitler's genocidal collaborators as mere replicas of their Führer ignores the crucial importance of their personal motives. That these motives matter in the light of Marrus' question can be illustrated by a closer look at the organization chiefly responsible for Hitler's terror policies. Thus, Himmler and Heydrich recruited many of their leading Gestapo officials from among experienced CID men who had already proven their professional qualities during the Weimar Republic and who were far more concerned with the advancement of their careers than with any party-political ideology. The best known example in this respect was, of course, the infamous Gestapo chief who was to become Adolf Eichmann's superior in the Reichssicherheitshauptamt, Heinrich Müller.

Müller had entered the Munich Metropolitan Police at the age of 19, shortly after the end of World War I. He rapidly advanced in its political department, where he received the task of monitoring left-wing parties and earned a reputation as a particularly ruthless Communist-baiter. In 1933 Himmler and Heydrich recruited Müller for their newly established *Bayerische Politische Polizei* (the precursor of the Gestapo), in spite of the fact that Müller was no Nazi Party member. Indeed, he would – without much enthusiasm – only become one as late as 1939, when he became head of the Gestapo. A political evaluation report of two years earlier praised him for his draconic measures against the Communists during the Weimar era, but tellingly added:

> It is no less clear, however, that had it been his task, Müller would have proceeded just the same against the Right. With his vast ambition and relentless drive, he would have done anything to win the appreciation of whoever might be boss in a given system.

For this reason, the Ortsgruppenleiter of Munich-Pasing had observed about Müller, somewhat earlier: 'We cannot very well imagine him as a party comrade.' And yet, only a few years later this unwelcome party comrade belonged to the elite circle of Hitler's extermination experts.

Another example is Müller's colleague, Franz Josef Huber. If Müller's ruthless opportunism was frowned upon in party circles, Huber was originally considered an outright enemy of the Nazi movement. As Müller, he had been employed at the political department of the Munich CID before 1933. But whereas Müller had persecuted the left, Huber's 'victims' were on the right side of the political spectrum. In a fiercely critical party evaluation report of 1937, Huber is said to have been an informer on Nazi colleagues during the Weimar years and even to have referred to Hitler as a 'runaway, unemployed house-painter' and an 'Austrian deserter'. Hardly surprising then, Huber was scheduled to be executed after the Nazi's came to power. Heydrich saved him by offering him a post in his police force. Huber finally wound up as Gestapo chief of Vienna.[19]

For the moment these two examples may suffice to underline the caution required when identifying the motives of the perpetrators. For it is by no means self-evident to assume 'idealist' intentions with Hitler's genocidal collaborators solely on the basis of their involvement in the crime. Without doubt, Huber and particularly Müller belonged to the leading men of this group. But their motives appear to have remained at a fair distance from the paranoid ones discussed earlier. Apparently, others could be at least as inspiring.

But the most important objection against the patho-ideological perspective remains its paradoxical exoneration of the perpetrators. Inspired by their revolting crimes, the advocates of the Laoconian point of view underscore their profound evil by picturing them as the blinded and obsessively fanaticized disciples of Hitler's satanic *Weltanschauung*. Inevitably however, the result of such a picture is the opposite of the painter's intention. For with his violent brush strokes, the criminals he seeks to expose transform into the psychopathic crusaders of their Führer's gospel. In this way, the Nazi criminal acquires the amalgamated characteristics of the bogeyman, the demon and the lunatic. But with the appearance of this pitch-black diabolical culprit, the possibility of identification, and thus worldly judgment, evaporates into thin air. For how, after all, should we be able to judge those who considered themselves as 'latter-day Laocoöns in the grip of a death struggle', or who genuinely felt that the indiscriminate mass killing of men, women and children equaled the rescue of the world or the extermination of vermin on the field? One can hardly reproach the agonized Laocoön for defending himself, or the family man for protecting his loved ones and the farmer for assuring the survival of his crops. The problem here is, of course, that all three lack any sense of wrong-doing. And because of this, the attribution of subjective guilt becomes impossible. For guilt presupposes blame, which in turn requires the ability to distinguish between right and wrong. With the absence of the latter, the first two become meaningless.

Whoever takes the patho-ideological interpretation seriously is therefore confronted by the uneasy outcome that the only remaining yardstick left for passing judgment on the Nazi killers is the one we normally reserve for the mentally ill and insane. If the criminal acts of such unfortunates result from their mental deficiency we do not consider them subjectively guilty and therefore do not punish them, but instead refer them to an asylum for appropriate care and treatment. Paradoxically then, the application of the patho-ideological perspective to the collaborators of Hitler's genocide inevitably results in the excuse of their conduct, as one simply cannot diagnose the patient as mentally deficient and then call him to account for the actions caused by his handicap. In such a scenario individual guilt and criminal responsibility disappear behind the horizon of mental derangement and the Nazi genocide itself is reduced to an error of judgment with the gas chambers as the absolute low point of its catastrophic consequences. According to this kind of logic, the mass murders are indeed turned into a self-defense strategy of the Third Reich, which may not have had any basis in reality, but which, in the final analysis, becomes understandable – and even excusable – because of the failing mental capabilities of those who carried them out.

Such considerations may well have played a part in Von dem Bach's statement before the IMT, and, as we shall see, they initially determined the defense of some of his former SS colleagues.[20] But there can be no doubt that they are not the intention of the advocates of the patho-ideological interpretation of the perpetrators' conduct. And yet, they form its logical outcome. Thus we arrive at the bizarre situation in which the very same arguments applied by the Nuremberg defense counsel to exonerate their clients were subsequently adopted by their 'historical prosecutors' to emphasize the exact opposite.

3 The Laocoön in Nuremberg

The idea that the behavior of the Nazi killers could somehow be explained by a perverted form of 'subjective self-defense', based on erroneous ideological assumptions – the very heart of the patho-ideological interpretation –, was already thoroughly dealt and dispensed with shortly after the war. The clearest demonstration of its inadequacy took place in the Nuremberg court room during one of the so-called follow-up trials by the Americans. It concerned the Einsatzgruppen-trial in 1947/48, in which this particular scenario of self-defense played a significant role.[21] On trial were a number of commanding officers of the mobile annihilation units of the SS – the Einsatzgruppen –, who had carried out mass killing operations in Eastern Europe and the Soviet territories. Because of the overwhelming evidence none of the defendants seriously denied his objective participation in these killings. Disagreement, however, arose over their *subjective* involvement. Thus, their defense counsel sought to convince the judges that their clients had actually committed their crimes in good faith. While recognizing that in reality their victims had constituted no threat at all to either themselves or the German Reich, they maintained that the defendants had nevertheless genuinely believed in the existence of such a threat at the time and had acted accordingly. Clearly, in hindsight, they were proved wrong, but considering the circumstances they could hardly be blamed for this 'judgmental error'. In the words of the prominent legal expert, Professor Reinhart Maurach, this defense reads as follows:

> The defendants, according to the National Socialist theory as well as due to their own conception and experience, were obsessed with a psychological delusion based on a fallacious idea concerning the identity of the aims of Bolshevism and the political role of Jewry in Eastern Europe. This conception was apt not only to exclude the possibility of a discussion regarding the moral defensibility of the liquidation order but to bring the defendants to the conviction that the attack against the future existence of the German Reich and people was to be expected mainly from the Jewish population in the occupied Russian territories.

Based on these arguments, leading defense counsel Dr. Rudolf Aschenauer insisted that the defendants had committed their criminal acts 'in presumed self-defense on behalf of a third party', and 'under conditions of presumed necessity to act for the rescue of a third party from immediate, otherwise unavoidable danger.' The 'third party' here was, of course, made up of the

German Reich and its people, whose very existence was supposedly endangered by Eastern European Jewry. And, as Aschenauer continued, 'if the existence of the state or of the nation is directly threatened, then any citizen ... may act for their protection.' That the menace did not really exist hardly mattered as far as the judgment on the defendants was concerned, for 'An error concerning the prerequisites of self-defense or of an act for the protection of a third party is to be treated as an error about facts and constitutes ... a legal excuse or – at the very least – a mitigating circumstance.'

The striking parallel between this line of defense by Aschenauer and his colleagues on the one hand, and the patho-ideological perspective of historians such as Dawidowicz and Goldhagen on the other, can hardly escape anyone. And the resemblance is even more remarkable when one realizes that the intentions behind both positions are diametrically opposed to one another. Thus, although the arguments used to explain the behavior of the perpetrators are identical, the Nuremberg defense counsel used them to emphasize the innocence of their clients, whereas the historians apply them to underline the exact opposite. As far as logical consistency is concerned, the latter are obviously no match for the lawyers, but this did not benefit their clients much.

In what was a surprisingly humorous rejoinder, given the subject matter under consideration, presiding judge Michael A. Musmanno reduced the subjective self-defense argument to the obvious nonsense it was:

> Under this state of law a citizen of Abyssinia could proceed to Norway and there kill a Norwegian on the basis that he, the Abyssinian, was motivated only by the desire to protect his country from an assumed aggression by the Norwegian.
> And that is not all – ....
> Thus, if the Abyssinian mentioned above, invaded Norway out of assumed necessity to protect his nation's interest, but it developed later that he killed the wrong person, he would be absolved because he had simply made a mistake.

That Musmanno and his fellow judges had little sympathy with such sophistry was made crystal-clear in their conclusion:

> The annihilation of the Jews had nothing to do with the defence of Germany, the genocide program was in no way connected with the protection of the Vaterland, it was entirely foreign to the military issue. Thus, taking into consideration all that has been said in this particular phase of the defence, the Tribunal concludes that the argument that the Jews in themselves constituted an aggressive menace to

Germany, a menace which called for their liquidation in self-defence, is *untenable as being opposed to all facts, all logic and all law*.²²

The very idea that the defendants – all of sound mind and in possession of a level of intelligence and education considerably above average – had committed their crimes because they had genuinely believed in such a factual, logical and legal absurdity, was simply too grotesque for credibility. And in its verdict, the court again made it clear that it was not prepared to follow Aschenauer and his colleagues in this. Out of the twenty-two officers who stood trial, it sentenced no less than fourteen to death, two to life imprisonment and five to sentences between ten and twenty years.²³

What the Einsatzgruppen-trial then made clear at a very early stage already, was that the notion of a misguided ideological obsession on the part of the Nazi mass murderers was untenable, not only because it formed such a bizarre contrast with common sense considerations and historical facts, but particularly also because it did not match the profile of its representatives in the dock. Contrary to the suggestions of their counsel, these defendants were no deranged 'idealists' who had lost their grip on reality and should therefore be excused for their crimes. Whatever their motives for participation in the mass extermination might have been, a blind belief in its justified necessity was not among them.

In an even more dramatic fashion, a lesson of at least similar significance was spelled out in yet another trial against a major Nazi criminal, some fifteen years later. This time it took place in Jerusalem and was directed against one of the chief coordinators of Hitler's genocidal bureaucracy, Adolf Eichmann. As head of Department IV B 4 of the RSHA, Eichmann had organized the mass deportation transports of Jews from the occupied countries to the extermination camps in Poland. His arrest by the Israeli secret service was clearly a formidable catch and his abduction from Argentina in order to bring him before a court of law was generally applauded as an act of supreme justice. Here, after all, was a Nazi criminal who had played a decisive role in the operational heart of the annihilation machinery and whose criminal reputation ranked only slightly below that of its main architects, Himmler, Heydrich and Müller. Here too, was the man, who, as we saw earlier, had shown himself particularly cheerful over the fact that he had personally been involved in the murder of millions.

Considering Eichmann's prominent role in these killings, it was therefore hardly surprising that one of his many instant biographers dubbed him 'the most sadistic and callous murderer of men, women and children this world has ever known.'[24] And indeed, as more and more details surfaced about the murderous involvement of this former 'expediter of death', as he was called by some of his colleagues, Eichmann grew into the very embodiment of criminal perversion. On the eve of his trial in Jerusalem, Dutch author and trial reporter Harry Mulisch accurately captured the widely felt drama of the moment when he wrote:

> It is one of the most fantastic somersaults of history that this trial will be held in Jerusalem. In that same city a man has been sentenced of whom the mysterious story goes that he has taken 'the sins of men upon himself'. Now there is a man on trial who is supposed to have committed all of them.[25]

The image of Eichmann's trial as the counterpart of that against Jesus certainly reflected much of the high-strung expectations over Eichmann's performance before his judges. But, as with the earlier Jerusalem trial, the court room's public met with a grave disappointment. For as the carpenter's son from Nazareth had hardly lived up to the image of God's Son, neither did the chicken farmer and Mercedes Benz employee from Buenos Aires showed much resemblance with the devil's envoy. Thus, the anxiously awaited exposure of the super villain and the meticulous dissection of his diabolical mind and character turned into an outright disillusion from the moment Eichmann entered the court room on 11 April, 1961. For instead of showing the particulars of a demon in disguise, the criminal inside the Jerusalem dock turned out to be of a breath-taking human mediocrity. As one trial observer put it, it was 'the discovery that there was nothing to discover' which turned the Eichmann trial into such a shocking experience.[26]

The paradoxical features of the trial could indeed hardly have been greater. Here was a man on trial for organizing millionfold murder, who, when questioned, was unable to produce anything more than inarticulate and stereotyped answers and cliché-ridden pseudo-justifications which were so utterly devoid of meaning that they almost became laughable. Without doubt, Eichmann's appeal to Kant's categorical imperative was the culmination of his farcical courtroom performance. As trial reporter Hannah Arendt commented: 'Despite all the efforts of the prosecution, everybody could see that this man was not a "monster", but it was difficult indeed not to suspect that he was a clown.'[27]

The greatest shock of the Eichmann trial was not the obvious impossibility of matching crime and punishment, but the bizarre discrepancy between the format of the crime and that of the criminal. Personified by the man in the glass booth, this discrepancy turned the logic of evil upside down by demonstrating that, apparently, one did not need to be a psychopathic megalomaniac to find satisfaction in murdering millions of people. It was Hannah Arendt who most aptly captured the lesson by subtitling her trial report with the famous formula of 'the banality of evil'. But the phenomenon itself was neither new nor limited to this particular SS officer. It had already been apparent in the courtrooms of Nuremberg and elsewhere, and it would surface again and again in the subsequent German trials against Hitler's genocidal collaborators.

4 The carrousel of fate

It was certainly no coincidence that Eichmann's banality manifested itself so clearly in the courtroom. The sobering reduction of evil to common human proportions forms a standard ingredient of most criminal trials and the German ones against the collaborators of the Nazi state were no exception. The defendants in these trials were no mythical characters, but specimens of the kind, persons of flesh and blood, who were called to account for their involvement in concrete criminal acts. That their prosaic courtroom appearances differed considerably from the more flamboyant presentations of historical imagination is therefore hardly surprising. For anyone who seriously wants to find out why these men (and women) had once 'followed Hitler on his murderous path', however, it is imperative to study their 'courtroom profiles'. For they document a significantly more mundane – even though by no means more reassuring – story than the Laoconian-style historiography. Thus, to get to know these criminals and their backgrounds one has to turn to those who brought them to justice during the past decades. They consisted of the criminal investigators, state prosecutors and especially also the judges, who got to know them far more intimately than any historian ever would. For a variety of reasons, the efforts and achievements of these prosecution officials have met with considerable criticism, which can easily be summed up by the simple threefold formula of 'too little, too late and too lenient'. Such reproaches were targeted particularly at the track record of the West German justice system, and for each of them serious arguments can be found.[28] Paradoxically however, it is precisely this much criticized West German justice system which has taught us by far the most about the backgrounds, the psychology and modus operandi of these criminals. And there are three main reasons for this.

The first consists of the relatively demanding legal obligation for West German courts to motivate extensively and explicitly the considerations and decisions on which their judgments and verdicts are based. For this reason, these judgments are far more informative to the investigator than those by, say, Dutch, East German or Anglo-American courts. The second reason relates to the fact that of all criminal justice systems which dealt with Nazi criminals, the West German one took by far the greatest interest in the (subjective) background of their conduct. And this too resulted in observations and insights of considerable value to historical and criminological research into the question of their motivation. The third reason why, in particular, the West German documentation on the post-war prosecution and trials of Nazi crimes is so informative to us is probably the most surprising one. For as far as the gravest Nazi crimes were concerned, it lasted some fifteen years before any systematic prosecution policy was set up in West-Germany, with the establishment of the Central Office for the Investigation of Nazi Crimes in Ludwigsburg. As a result of this 'delayed' judicial reaction, the perpetrators of these crimes were given every opportunity to re-integrate into post-war German society without much difficulty. And the smooth nature of their 'return to normalcy' underscores one of the most crucial insights into the criminological profile of Hitler's genocide collaborators: its inconspicuous middle-class character.

Before 1933 none of them had even the faintest idea of the criminal career he (or she) would make in the service of their Führer. And the very thought that in ten years' time they would consist of routine participants in mass murder was as unimaginable to them as to any of their fellow countrymen. Under normal circumstances then, hardly any of them would have turned criminal and in their biographies one looks in vain for characteristics which somehow seem to have preordained them for their role as Hitler's mass executioners. With rare exceptions, none had criminal antecedents or suffered from any certifiable personality disorder which could offer even the beginning of an explanation for their criminal conduct. At the time of this conduct, most were married, headed a family and belonged to either the Catholic or Protestant church communities of which more than 90 % of the German population were members. And despite the fiercely anti-clerical stance of the Nazi movement and the regime, we know that a substantial number of them stuck to their religious convictions and church membership. No different from the average German citizen then, they had been brought up with the elementary notions of right and wrong, on the basis of which they had developed a moral awareness which determined their regular day-to-day behavior within society. What set them apart from their fellow citizens, however, and what finally landed them in court, was that, at some point in their lives, they had chosen to abandon this awareness of right and wrong as a guide-line for their conduct, and to offer their services to a government with a distinctly criminal agenda. It is this choice which brought them on the murderous path of Hitler's *Unrechtsstaat* and which calls for further investigation if one seeks a serious answer to Marrus' puzzling question.

Whoever undertakes such an investigation on the basis of the prosecution records referred to earlier, will discover that the answer to the puzzle lies above all in the *absence* of distinctive features of those who fill its pages. For they were indeed distinctive because of the crimes of which they stood accused, but hardly because of their unusual personalities or background characteristics. In fact, it is no exaggeration to say that most would never have exceeded their inconspicuousness if historical coincidence had not 'tapped them on the shoulder', so to speak. And we can get a pretty good idea what this 'shoulder tap' looked like when focusing on the recruits for Hitler's earliest mass murderous enterprise: the so-called *Euthanasie-Aktion*.

This wholesale medical killing program targeted Germany's physically and mentally handicapped and was set up by Hitler's personal Chancellery at the start of the war. It lasted until its very end and cost a total of some 200.000 lives. The patients included in this secret program – men, women and children – were murdered either through carbon-monoxide gassing in one of the six extermination centers spread across Germany, or poisoned by means of lethal injections or overdosed medication in 'regular' nursing homes.[29] The first – gassing – phase of this 'mercy killing' project provided considerable expertise for Hitler's subsequent genocidal operations in Poland and the Soviet Union and part of its staff was later transferred to the so-called *Aktion Reinhard* camps, Belzec, Treblinka and Sobibor, where about one-third of all Jewish victims of the Holocaust perished under its hands.

One of the obvious questions in any attempt to make sense out of this group of annihilation experts concerns the way in which they became involved in Hitler's killing apparatus. Dietrich Allers, one of the leading managers of this so-called T4 organization (named after its Berlin address, *Tiergartenstrasse* 4), pictured his introduction as follows:

> I was scheduled to go to officer's training school, but then, in November 1940, my mother met Werner Blankenburg in the street in Berlin. When she told him what I was doing he said, "That's ridiculous. There is an opening in my department for a lawyer. I'll fix it." And that's how I got into T4.[30]

Such a dreary prologue to a profession as prominent administrator of mass killing may well appear too ridiculous to be taken seriously, but there is actually no reason to doubt Allers' version in this respect. Just as with many of his generation, the start of the war meant the unwelcome end of a promising civil career. In Allers' case it was that of a young lawyer in Prussian public service. Instead, he was now drafted and stationed in Poland as a non-commissioned officer with the task of training recruits. Unsurprisingly, he felt little enthusiasm about his new duties and his mother's coincidental meeting with his old SA-comrade – Allers had joined both the NSDAP and the SA as a law student in 1932 – offered him an excellent opportunity to escape from his dreaded military existence. Werner Blankenburg had worked himself up to the position of deputy to the operational chief of the 'euthanasia' organization, Viktor Brack. And it was indeed a fact that, at the time, the bureau was in desperate need of an experienced legal professional, as the first one had resigned after a fierce dispute.[31] Allers, therefore, did not need to think twice before deciding to accept Blankenburg's offer. The opportunity to leave the military behind, return home and pick up his profession in the service of such a prestigious institute as the Führer Chancellery, was certainly more than he could have dreamed of. And so, as of January 1941, Dietrich Allers started to devote his talents to the administrative aspects of the annihilation program.

Allers' unspectacular and coincidental introduction to T4 was hardly exceptional. As he himself told his post-war interviewer, it applied to most of the organization's employees:

> I was always of the opinion that most people got in through connections. They would hear of the job as being "attached to the Führer Chancellery" and that sounded good. Then of course these jobs carried extra pay; and it meant not having to go to the front.[32]

Again, there is no reason to distrust Allers on this point, for the post-war criminal records of the organization's staff show that the T4 organization was indeed to an amazing degree a syndicate of friends, acquaintances and relatives. Thus, Allers' colleague (and co-defendant) Reinhold Vorberg thanked his appointment as head of its 'transport service' (responsible for carrying the selected death candidates to the gassing centers) to his cousin, T4-chief Brack. And his successor was yet another cousin, engineer Gerhardt Siebert. There were also family ties between the bureau's financial wizard, Hans-Joachim Becker, and Dr. Herbert Linden, one of the main organizers of the killing program. Although it is not entirely clear whether it was Linden who actually recruited Becker for T4, the fact is that the two men got along very well. After Becker's start with Brack's bureau, he lived for a while in the household of his brother-in-law, and the two men joined forces in their attempt to save Becker's epileptic sister from Hitler's 'euthanasia' regime. '*Millionen*-Becker' was the one who turned T4 into a highly profitable enterprise by his introduction of a clever cost-manipulation system, whereby the patients who had already been gassed and cremated were 'kept alive' in an administrative sense so that huge sums of money could be earned with their 'continued' care and feeding.[33]

The head of the central finance office, accountant Friedrich Lorent, was no relative of Brack but an old acquaintance. During the mid-nineteen thirties, the two men had been office neighbors in Berlin and Brack had supported Lorent during a fierce conflict with an SA leader. In the autumn of 1941 Lorent worked as manager of a former Polish company in building materials in Warsaw, a job he allegedly detested because of the chaos and corruption surrounding the German administration of confiscated Polish-Jewish property. While on leave in Berlin, in the winter of 1941/42, Lorent visited Brack and complained about his situation. Brack instantaneously offered him a job at his bureau with the words '*Du, ich brauche Dich*'

['You, I need you']. As head of the finance office, Lorent succeeded two other friends of Brack, Willy Schneider and Fritz Schmiedel. Schneider had earlier introduced his cousin, bookkeeper Alfred Ittner, to the organization. In April 1942, Ittner was dispatched to Sobibor.[34]

Among the regular customers of Berlin nightclub waiter Franz Rum was the co-organizer of the killing program which specifically targeted handicapped children ('*Kinder-Euthanasie*'), Richard von Hegener. When the nightclub business deteriorated due to the restrictions imposed by the war, Rum looked around for other employment. Von Hegener helped him to a job at the photography section of T4, where the files and pictures of the murdered victims were copied. After a while, however, Rum became allergic to the chemicals used in the process. He asked for other work, 'preferably in the open air', as his judges echoed the defendant in their trial judgment. This could be arranged: Rum was offered a new job in a 'labor camp' in Poland. It turned out to be Treblinka.[35]

The brothers Franz and Josef Wolf took over the photo shop in the Czechoslovakian town of Krummau after their father's death in 1938. Both came to T4 a few years later through the introduction of their fellow townsman Franz Wagner, who already worked at the bureau's photo department and who knew the Wolf brothers from the time he was an apprentice in their father's shop. In March 1943, the brothers were transferred to Sobibor. Wagner turned out to be a prolific recruiter for T4 among his townsmen for he also introduced the Krummau tailor Franz Suchomel to the organization. In August 1942, Suchomel was sent to Treblinka.[36]

And then, there was the CID man from the Austrian town of Linz, Franz Stangl. We will have ample opportunity to get to know him better later on, but he too was among those who came to T4 through 'friendly intervention'. Thus, Stangl got along badly with his Gestapo chief and was on the lookout for other employment when a former colleague and fellow student from the CID school offered to introduce him to the secret government organization where he himself already worked in what he described as a 'pleasant job'. Stangl gratefully accepted and came as a policeman to the Hartheim extermination center, and, later on, to Sobibor and Treblinka.[37]

Those who did not find their way to T4 through this informal network of relatives and friends were generally recruited on the basis of what the Berlin historian and trial expert Wolfgang Scheffler called the 'coincidence principle'.[38] A striking example is that of the five young girls (aged between seventeen and twenty years), who became responsible for the registration of the murdered patients and their 'possessions' in the Hartheim and Grafeneck extermination centers. They also drew up the transport lists and typed the thousands of 'comfort letters' which were sent to the relatives of the murdered victims, including fabricated data on the circumstances of their deaths and falsified names of the doctors involved in their 'care'. Three of these girls were trainees at the *Defaka*, or *Deutsches Familien Kaufhaus* (German Family Department Store) and were simply drafted by the Frankfurt labor exchange. This also happened with the fourth, who was a shop-girl in a Frankfurt store, whereas the fifth was simply conscripted by the Party Gauleitung shortly after passing her school exams. None of these women had a political profile beyond that of a membership of the 'German Girl's League', the 'National Socialist Welfare Organization', or the 'German Labor Front.'[39]

No less coincidental was the recruitment of the Westphalian farmer's and miller's son August Miete. From 1921 onwards, he and his brother ran the farm their father had left them. In the spring of 1940, however, August considered it time to start on his own and – equipped with a recently acquired Nazi Party membership card – requested the Agricultural Chamber in Münster to grant him his own agricultural settlement. Unfortunately, they could not help him, but as an alternative they offered him a position at the estate of the Grafeneck institution. Miete accepted and, from May 1940 until October 1941, tended the farm lands of this gassing center, after which he was transferred to another one at Hadamar. Here, he worked as a so-called *Brenner* in the institute's crematorium where the bodies of the gassed victims were burned. In June 1942, Miete came to Treblinka, where, because of his brutal conduct, he turned into a much feared member of the camp's staff.[40]

The Münster Agricultural Chamber also recruited the thirty-six years old dairy master Willi Mentz for T4. Since 1929 Mentz had worked in the dairy business but in early 1940 he applied for a job with the police. They could not use him there, but considering his profession the Münster agency offered him 'something better', namely a job at Grafeneck. Mentz accepted, and – just like Miete – was informed of what went on there and sworn to secrecy. According to his admission, he tended the Grafeneck livestock for the next one-and-a-half year and was then – as Miete – transferred to Hadamar, where he divided his time between work in the vegetable garden and the maintenance of the central heating system. Like Miete, Mentz came to Treblinka in the summer of 1942, where he acquired a similar reputation of brutality.[41]

This certainly also applied to carpenter Karl Frenzel, whose involvement with T4 was the result of nothing less than his procreative abilities. Thus, around Christmas 1939, Frenzel was discharged from Wehrmacht service as a so-called *kinderreicher Familienvater* (father of a large family). His biological declaration of loyalty to a regime which celebrated the family as the 'germ cell of the nation' not only earned his wife a (bronze) medal hailing her motherhood, but also rewarded her husband with suspension of his military duties. This, however, was not at all to Frenzel's liking as he genuinely enjoyed these duties and now felt embarrassed in front of his comrades and his two brothers, both of whom served in the Wehrmacht. And so, Frenzel immediately reported himself again as a volunteer and enlisted the support of his SA superiors to endorse his request. But Hitler's family policy was no joking matter and Frenzel received no reply. Instead, his SA chiefs suggested him to report to the Führer Chancellery in Berlin, which was looking for 'trustworthy party comrades for a special assignment'. Frenzel complied and, in January 1940, together with another fifteen T4 recruits, was informed in Berlin by Brack and Blankenburg about his new duties and sworn to secrecy. He worked – *inter alia* as crematorium worker – in the gassing centers Grafeneck, Hadamar and Bernburg, and came to Sobibor in April 1942.[42]

We could extend this list of T4 recruiting examples without much difficulty, but it should be clear by now that Scheffler accurately described the recruitment policies of the killing organization as being largely governed by coincidence. Indeed, if Allers' mother had not bumped into Werner Blankenburg during her daily shopping round in Berlin, it is highly unlikely that her son would ever have come into contact with the mass extermination business. And if they would have granted August Miete his farm, had accepted Willi Mentz with the police force and had allowed Karl Frenzel his return to the military, the first would have continued his peasant existence, whereas Mentz and Frenzel would have worn the police uniform and the field gray of the Wehrmacht, respectively. None of these four men had actively sought a career in the killing profession and with respect to

Miete, Mentz and Frenzel one could say that it was not even their 'first choice.' Their entry into Hitler's annihilation machinery then was not the outcome of careful deliberation on the pros and cons of employment in the extermination business, but the result of a chance meeting between fate and opportunity. And for their colleagues this was little different.

Prior to their enrolment in T4 none of them had any idea of its existence, let alone its purpose. Different from the doctors and nurses who were to lend their hand in the 'euthanasia' killings, hardly any of them had ever personally visited a psychiatric ward, nursing home or insane asylum and it is highly doubtful whether they had any understanding of (or interest in) their government's intention with its inhabitants. Typical in this respect was perhaps Reinhold Vorberg's reaction when cousin Brack promoted him to head of T4's transport service. When Brack explained its purpose, Vorberg reportedly answered him that he had no idea what the concept of euthanasia stood for and that he couldn't understand why, in times of war, one should bother with '*die Verrückten*' ['the lunatics'].[43]

Of course, one could still suspect that T4 selected its staff by political criteria, i.e. that the recruitment of the men described here was somehow related to their Nazi profile. And it is certainly true that all of the above were members of the NSDAP or any of its branch organizations. But neither their grounds for entry (often linked to 'economic', career-related considerations), nor their commitment to the Party organizations of which they were members (none of them occupied a particularly profiled position within these organizations) can really explain for their selection. That T4 primarily recruited its collaborators from within the circle of Party comrades seems understandable enough, but why exactly it chose *these* ones from among the millions of candidates can only be explained through the use of the social network described earlier, combined with random selection.[44]

This even applies to such a notorious T4 criminal as the Stuttgart Kriminalkommissar Christian Wirth, who would play a leading role in both the 'euthanasia' killing program as well as in its successor, the *Aktion Reinhard*. His former colleague, Dietrich Allers, had this to say about the ratio behind Wirth's recruitment for T4:

> I am sure that when Grafeneck [the first extermination centre at which Wirth was appointed 'office chief', close to the CID bureau in Stuttgart where he was

employed, DdM] was opened up and they needed a couple of police officers to put in charge, whoever was the chief of police in that district simply said "You and you" – and one of them was Wirth. Perhaps it was because he was a tough sort of man his superiors thought him capable of doing a difficult job; but it wasn't a matter of careful or scientific selection of these people.[45]

And if we may believe the same witness, their motives for acceptance were no less trivial and lacking in 'inner conviction' than the grounds for their selection. Invariably, these motives rooted in a common concern for the (im)material advantages associated with T4 employment. That is to say, they consisted of such conventional incentives as concern for jobs, income and status, as well as the welcome perspective of being exempted from military service in times of war. One could call this ordinary opportunism, and that is in fact pretty much what it was.

5 The opportunist route to crime (and back)

That something as trite as common self-interest could serve as the prime motivation for participation in mass murder may be considered too meager an explanation. And yet, everyone knows how potent an incentive opportunism can be, even in societies which we would generally consider to be liberal, diversified, democratic and free. In social environments with an authoritarian, dictatorial or totalitarian ruling system, however, its prevalence as a behavior governing principle is obviously even more manifest. Here, opportunism becomes a veritable way of life for anyone but the incorrigible rebel at all costs. And it is precisely because of these costs that the latter's presence is quite rare in such societies. Thus, under the circumstances prevailing in the Third Reich opportunism became the supreme ally of its criminal regime. Far more than the personal idiosyncrasies of its collaborators, these circumstances form the true key to Michael Marrus' puzzle, and their impact can again be studied particularly well within the context of Hitler's *Euthanasie-Aktion*.

To Hitler, his medical assassination program was more than the fulfilment of a long cherished wish; it was the ultimate test for his claim to unconditional power. For with the inauguration of this program on the day of his invasion of Poland, he crossed a threshold which he had eschewed until then. In 1935 Hitler had already informed his inner circle that, in case of war, he would settle the 'euthanasia question' as public opposition to it would be less prominent and easier to tackle than in normal times.⁴⁶ Obviously, two years after his appointment to Reich Chancellor he still could not trust the German people to support his extermination agenda. Indeed, only a few months earlier, his own Minister of Justice, National-Conservative Franz Gürtner, had informed his staff in no unclear terms that any form of state-organized euthanasia remained unacceptable: 'If we would start out in this direction, it would touch on the very foundation of Christianity's teachings to humanity; it would be the fulfilment of Nietzschean thoughts.'⁴⁷ Consequently, in the final report of the Ministerial Committee for the Revision of the Penal Code of 1936, any suggestions in this 'Nietzschean' sense were dismissed out of hand: 'There can be no question of an authorization of the extermination of so-called life-unworthy life.' Thus, the committee concluded that forced sterilization was to remain the most drastic measure which the state was allowed in its combat against the 'degeneration within society':

> But the strength of the moral standard of the prohibition on killing should not be allowed to weaken through the provision of exemptions for victims of severe illnesses or accidents because of considerations of mere expediency, even if these unfortunate persons are still only related to society through their past or outward appearance.

And so it was to remain, in legal terms at least. For until the very end of Hitler's rule any form of euthanasia would continue to be forbidden by law.

For obvious reasons then, Gürtner and his department were kept in the dark when the extermination program was being set up by the Führer Chancellery in the summer of 1939. It was not until a year later that Gürtner received a photocopy (!) of the decree which had set the killings in motion. It consisted of a one-line note, dated September 1, 1939, and signed by Hitler:

> Reichsleiter Bouhler and Dr. Brandt, M.D., are charged with the responsibility of enlarging the authority of certain physicians, to be designated by name, so that persons who, according to human judgement, are incurable can, upon a most careful diagnosis of their condition of sickness, be accorded a mercy death.

By this time, however, Gürtner had already been informed of the killing practices which, based on Hitler's ruling, were taking place all over Germany. On 8 July 1940, he had received an extensive report by the guardianship judge of the Brandenburg court, Dr. Lothar Kreyssig. It mentioned murders which allegedly had taken place in the Hartheim nursing institute, near Linz. In his report, judge Kreyssig was very outspoken in his criticism on the perversion of justice under Nazism in general, as well as on Gürtner's acquiescing compliance with it. In accordance with their repugnant principle '*Recht ist was dem Volke nutzt*' ['Right is what benefits the people'], the Nazis had exempted entire areas of public life from the rule of law. Next to the concentration camps, this exemption now apparently also applied to the psychiatric homes and nursing institutes. Kreyssig informed his minister that he considered it his 'undoubted duty' as a judge 'to uphold the law', and that – after formally asking his highest superior for advice in the matter – he was determined to act accordingly.

Even more detailed was the memorandum sent to Adolf Hitler in person a day earlier by the evangelical pastor Gerhard Braune. For several months, Braune, vice-president of the Central Committee of the Inner Mission of the German Evangelical Church, had collected information on the state-organized mistreatment and killing of patients in a great many nursing institutes as well as in extermination centers such as Brandenburg, Grafeneck and Hartheim.[48] Three days after dispatching his memorandum, Braune, together with two of his sympathizers, informed Gürtner in a private meeting on his findings. As he recalled after the war, Gürtner was shocked:

> I clearly remember the first sentence of his reaction: "For a Reich Minister of Justice it is a fatal occurrence when it is reported to him by the most trustworthy of sources: 'in your Reich murders are constantly taking place and you know nothing of it!'" He thereupon spoke extensively on the unlawfulness of such measures, completely shared our views on the lawlessness and sinfulness of such a state of affairs.... We were surprised to find such a complete understanding for our protest with him, a member of the Reich government. He promised to help us.[49]

Kreyssig's request for counsel and Braune's alarming information compelled Gürtner to take action, and so did the incoming reports from his own attorneys general. Among them was one from the state prosecutor of Stuttgart, who forwarded an anonymous murder complaint concerning the killing of mental patients, adding that he had heard of 'several similar, unbelievable rumors' lately. Thus, he enquired 'whether he should initiate criminal investigations and ask for assistance from the '*Geheime Staatspolizei*'.

Prompted by these alarming reports, Gürtner requested a meeting with the head of the Reich Chancellery, Hans Lammers, insisting that the reported killings should be terminated, or at the very least be given a lawful basis. On July 23, Lammers informed Gürtner on the *Aktion* and told him that Hitler had rejected any legal settlement. Lammers then asked Gürtner to send him all reports on the issue which had been sent to his ministry. Gürtner immediately complied, adding the following note:

> As you have told me yesterday, the Führer has refused to promulgate a law. In my opinion this implies the necessity to put an immediate stop to the secret killing of mentally ill patients. Not least because of the attempted concealment, the current state of affairs has become known rapidly and in wide circles. To what embarrassments this leads, I ask you to conclude from the enclosed appendixes. The number of such requests will multiply.
>
> It is extraordinarily precarious to answer to them in a formal manner, as neither the fact itself nor the contents of a decree from the Führer can be made public. With regard to its own subordinate agencies, the position that the Reich Ministry of Justice is ignorant of the entire state of affairs is utterly impossible.

What followed were a few meetings between Gürtner and the chief of the Führer Chancellery, Philipp Bouhler. On August 27, Bouhler handed Gürtner the photocopy of Hitler's decree, which listed him – Bouhler – as one of Hitler's two 'mercy killing' plenipotentiaries. This effectively ended Gürtner's opposition. During the next days he still made some feeble attempts to persuade Bouhler to at least regulate the killing campaign in accordance with formal procedures, but his efforts were in vain. On September 5, the KdF chief informed the minister in no uncertain terms who was calling the shots:

> On the basis of the Führer's proxy, I have, as the sole person responsible for the execution of the planned measures, given my staff the instructions which I considered essential. I do not find it necessary to issue special, written executive regulations in addition to that.[50]

For Gürtner, his confrontation with the Führer decree exhausted all possibilities to prevent the killings. Now that they proved to be based on the expressed wish of the supreme head of the Nazi state, they were to be considered 'legal'. Such, at least, was the conclusion Gürtner and his Under-Secretary of State, Franz Schlegelberger, reached on the decree after 'extensive combined investigation of the legal nature of the document', as Schlegelberger maintained decades later in his witness statement in a trial against a former 'mercy killing' specialist. Thus, after carefully weighing the pros and cons, the two government officials had decided that any action of the Führer's will possessed a lawful and binding status 'by virtue of the authority he had placed upon himself.'[51]

It is quite telling that Gürtner did not even take the trouble of enquiring with his cabinet chief (Hitler), for his attitude and that of his leading ministerial officials was symptomatic of the reaction the justice department had always shown when confronted with the criminal determination of the regime. Whether it concerned the crimes committed by the SA and SS against political opponents during its early, power consolidation days, the murders of the so-called *Röhm-Aktion* of June 30, 1934 (which Gürtner retrospectively sanctioned as lawful measures of state emergency, only a few days later), or the brutal conduct of Hitler's hordes during the pogrom night of 9/10 November 1938, again and again Gürtner and his ministry had bowed to political pressure. And this was in itself hardly surprising, since from the very beginning Gürtner's loyalty towards the *Rechtsstaat* had been severely limited by his conviction that this lawful and constitutional state should remain subordinate to 'national interests.' In an alliance with those who identified these interests with their criminal agenda, such flexibility in matters concerning the rule of law was bound to have fatal consequences.[52]

Among the victims of these consequences was the Brandenburg judge, Lothar Kreyssig. While awaiting his minister's directives, Kreyssig had in the meantime forbidden the psychiatric institutions under his jurisdiction, to discharge or hand over any of his pupils without his explicit approval. In addition, he had filed a murder complaint against 'mercy killing' plenipotentiary Bouhler with the prosecutor's office in Potsdam. In a private meeting with Gürtner, Kreyssig was now called to order for his actions. Gürtner showed him the photocopy of Hitler's decree and told Kreyssig that this settled the matter. But the judge would not budge, however, and replied that even if the document was authentic, it could never turn injustice into justice. Thus, he could not consider Hitler's decree as legally binding. Whereupon Gürtner responded: 'Yes, well, if you cannot recognize the will of the Führer as a legal source, you cannot remain a judge.' Shortly thereafter, Kreyssig was pensioned off.[53]

Gürtner's capitulation before the cold-blooded slaughter of Hitler's T4-*Aktion* was the absolute low point of the dismantling of the German *Rechtsstaat*, set in motion in 1933. To Hitler it signaled his triumph over the final institutional barrier which kept him from implementing his murderous agenda. Gürtner suddenly died after a brief illness, on 29 January 1941. It was left to Undersecretary Schlegelberger to endorse the judiciary's surrender and to implicate its leading officials in the crimes of their government. In April Schlegelberger assembled all attorneys general and presidents of the District Appeal Courts in Berlin, where they were informed on the 'euthanasia' – program by T4-chief Viktor Brack and the head of the organization's 'medical office', professor Werner Heyde. Without allowing for any discussion, Schlegelberger closed the meeting by concluding that 'in view of the existence of a legally valid Führer Decree, there could no longer be any objections against this measure.' Those present were instructed from now on to send all reports and complaints about the T4-operation – *'unbearbeitet'* [i.e. without taking any action] – to Schlegelberger's office. And so, state-organized murder became *de facto* legal.[54]

The effect of this self-imposed silence on Hitler's assassination project by the German judiciary on the collaborators of the project can hardly be overestimated. With the possible exception of the most simple-minded among them, they were all well aware of the fact that the killings to which they contributed constituted a violation of national German law. Indeed, they were even explicitly told as much at their introduction to T4, while the tight secrecy surrounding the killing project also left no doubt about its unlawful nature. Of course, this awareness was strongest with the doctors, psychiatrists and nurses, whose careers in health care went back to pre-Nazi times and who knew very well how controversial the subject of state-controlled euthanasia had always been, both inside and outside their professional circles. Among them, for example, was the protestant psychiatrist Carl Schneider, who, only two years before the Nazis came to power, had informed his colleagues in no uncertain terms of his principled opposition to any form of systematic, state-organized medical killing:

> Should a doctor be obliged in these instances to execute such a death sentence, or should it be the state's responsibility to compel the doctor to do so? Or is the state prepared to form a special class of professional executioners which carries out these matters? These considerations should be energetically brought to the attention of those in public office. It would imply that a certain group of doctors would have to be entrusted with it. *The medical profession would then not only be a profession of helpers, but also of executioners.*[55]

Only a few years later, Schneider sold his Hippocratic soul to the Nazi's for an academic chair at the University of Heidelberg, however, and showed himself perfectly willing to perform the role of medical executioner in Hitler's service. But not without a clear guarantee to legal immunity. As all T4-employees, he was promised such immunity by Hitler, but the Führer's authority was still not solid enough to avoid all doubts in this respect. This is hardly surprising as Hitler's assurance of exemption from criminal prosecution merely underlined the factual illegality of the 'euthanasia' program. And to Schneider as well as to many other potential collaborators, this remained a cause for some concern. It explains their repeated attempts to persuade Hitler to settle the 'mercy killing' project by law. These efforts failed, however, as Hitler refused and simply told his plenipotentiary Bouhler: 'My decree is law! I am state authority!'[56]

The success of such a claim to unchecked power obviously depended on the reaction of Hitler's environment, and more in particular of that of Gürtner and his judiciary. If the minister should decide to uphold the law of the land and instruct his attorneys general to act accordingly – i.e. to prosecute Hitler's 'mercy killers' – the Führer's self-crowned omnipotence would be unmasked as a despotic usurpation of power with unmistakably criminal intentions. Under the circumstances it seems perhaps unlikely that Gürtner and his men could have won such a confrontation. But it would certainly have caused considerable embarrassment for the regime and would have compelled its allies to choose openly between their loyalty to the laws of the Third Reich or to its de facto rulers. And this would at the very least have made their choice considerably more demanding. But the fact that Gürtner avoided the confrontation at all says enough about the moribund state of the German *Rechtsstaat* which he had himself helped to dismantle and undermine over the past years. His acceptance of Hitler's killing program was effectively its knock-out blow. For the Führer and his collaborators it removed the final hurdle on their road to mass murder.

The other two traditional advocates of public morality, the Roman Catholic and Protestant Churches, also shied away from an open confrontation over the issue. And for pretty much the same reasons. As their repeated collisions with Hitler's representatives over church- or religion-related questions illustrate, both Churches still possessed enough autonomous power and influence to make things difficult for the Nazi regime.[57]

Potentially, they had the moral authority to challenge Hitler's murder plans and thus, perhaps even to frustrate them. But their principled opposition to these plans did not lead to a unified and strong public protest as it was compromised by their essential support for the regime.[58] Illustrative in this respect were the reactions to pastor Braune and his sensational memorandum to Hitler:

> The official Church kept totally silent about it, even the official Inner Mission dared to do nothing.... After I had been sacked ... the treasurer of the Central Committee reproached me for exposing myself too much. One should not do that.[59]

It was only after Hitler's murder campaign had become a public secret that church leaders recalled their special responsibilities. But even then, their protests remained largely limited to carefully worded letters of objection to government officials, which not only came too late but were carefully kept from the public eye. This only changed with the courageous public address of the Münster bishop, Count Von Galen, nearly two years after the start of the killings. In his sermon on Sunday, August 3, 1941, Galen openly protested against the murders and announced his formal complaint with the police. His public protest made a profound impression and prompted Hitler to stop the gassings, a few weeks later. By this time, however, more than seventy thousand patients had already been murdered.[60]

Thus, through their prolonged silence over the murderous practices of their government, the German Churches also denied their public support to the opposition against these practices within society (and even within the Nazi movement itself[61]), and thereby smoothed the path for Hitler's executioners. As mentioned before, the majority of them were church members and many remained loyal – either openly or privately – to their churches even during the Nazi years. This applied, for example, to T4-recruit Karl Frenzel whom we met earlier on. Frenzel had his marriage consecrated, had all of his five children duly baptized and attended church with his wife 'every second Sunday or every three weeks.' Treblinka camp commander Franz Stangl, who had registered himself as '*gottgläubig*' ['God-believing', i.e. the Nazi term for those who still wished to register themselves as religious] as soon as his Gestapo-career made this preferable, nevertheless remained the solid Austrian Catholic he was by upbringing and tradition. And even the notorious Christian Wirth noted in his 1937 marriage application with the SS, that he and his bride-to-be were members of the *Evangelische Kirche*.[62]

Even if one were to assume that their church membership and their religious confession was inspired by habitual convention rather than by genuine personal conviction, the fact that, despite all Nazi propaganda to the contrary, they clung to it at all, suggests that they awarded some kind of moral significance to it. Put differently, it shows that, next to their revered Führer, they recognized still another 'moral authority' in their lives. Perhaps it would go too far to expect that a clear public protest from the Churches against Hitler's murder program would have kept them from participating in it. But again, it would have made their choice a great deal more difficult. As the (later) Federal Republic's Chancellor, Konrad Adenauer, put it shortly after the end of the war when addressing the co-responsibility of the Churches for the criminal policies of the Nazi regime:

> I believe that if the bishops had, jointly, in public and on a specific day, taken position against it from the pulpit, they could have prevented a great deal. That has not happened and there is no excuse for it.[63]

This was a clear statement from someone who could hardly be accused of belonging to the most uncompromising critics of his countrymen's accommodation under the Nazi regime. And it is difficult indeed to disagree with him. For just as Gürtner and his ministerial staff could have compelled the collaborators of the medical killing program to choose for or against the rules of law and justice, so the guardians of the Gospel could have forced them to decide between the commands of Christ and those of Hitler. Had they done so, it is certainly safe to assume that weighing the alternatives would indeed have been considerably more challenging for the choosers than it now actually was. For as both the judiciary and the Churches publicly betrayed their duties through their concerted silence, they were placed before the far less exacting task of opting in favor of those in power.

Thus, in the end, answering the question as to why so many followed Hitler down his murderous path is perhaps not as difficult as it seemed at first sight. Left with only their own moral compass in an environment exclusively controlled by the likes of Adolf Hitler, such a criminal route became the obvious choice for most. In a society in which the rule of injustice remained the only yardstick for guidance, traditional concepts of good and evil rapidly lost their meaning as directives for human conduct, particularly when such conduct was mobilized by the highest state authority. This does not imply that the murderers carried out their crimes with a 'lilywhite conscience', of course. It merely means that the inner voice of this conscience was no match for the interests at stake. As Hitler's accessories found no institutional echo of their reservations in the world around them, they were left to themselves to either heed or suppress such reservations. That most decided in favor of the latter can only be surprising to those who put their trust in a private moral integrity which is, however, virtually absent under the conditions prevailing in the *Unrechtsstaat*.[64] Our wholly justified admiration for the exceptions to this rule – of which Lothar Kreyssig forms an outstanding example –, is prompted by our sharp awareness that in such a state moral integrity is a rare quality indeed. As we demonstrated earlier on, for a government such as Hitler's the recruitment of collaborators willing to do anything under its authority was pretty much child's play.

And with the very same ease as with which they joined their Führer on his murderous path, his collaborators returned to the regular order of things as soon as he had left the stage. After spending a short time in captivity, most succeeded without too much difficulty in finding their way back to the social and occupational routine of their pre-war existence. Thus, only a month after Germany had surrendered, the infamous deputy camp commander of Treblinka, Kurt Franz, was already back at home with his wife in Düsseldorf. Immediately, he registered – under his own name – with the local employment agency and after three years working at construction sites, he again took up his old profession as a cook in 1949. Until his arrest ten years later, Franz worked in the kitchen of a restaurant at the Graf-Adolf-Platz, in the center of Düsseldorf. It was at short walking distance from the restaurants where he had acquired his gastronomic skills as a fifteen year old apprentice, some thirty years earlier. His Treblinka colleague, former nurse Otto Stadie, was also briefly in Düsseldorf in 1945, after his release by the Americans. A year later he settled in Nordenau, a small health resort in the Sauerland, some 175 kilometers to the east. Until his retirement in 1962 Stadie lived and worked here, both as a private nurse and as a souvenir selling shop assistant. Fellow nurse (and Treblinka comrade) Heinrich Matthes also succeeded in finding his way back to his old profession. After his release in 1945, he assisted briefly in clearing debris in the devastated city of Nuremberg. Soon however, he again devoted himself to the professional care of patients whom his previous employer had sentenced to death. Matthes ended his career as head nurse in a mental institution in Bayreuth.

In 1946, Treblinka's execution specialist Willi Mentz returned to the small village of Niedermeien, some 40 kilometers to the east of Bielefeld in North-Rhine Westphalia. Here, he took up his old profession as dairy master; a job which – with the interval of his T-4 career – he had performed since 1934. In 1952, however, he had to give up the dairy business as he fell ill from tuberculosis. Until his arrest in 1960, Mentz lived on disability benefit. After a brief stay in an American POW-camp near Munich, August Miete returned to the farm near Osnabrück which he had inherited from his father in 1921. In 1950 he exchanged his 'green collar' for a white one as he became manager of a local savings- and credit-bank until his arrest in May 1960. Former Sudeten-German tailor Franz Suchomel was also already a free man again in the summer months of 1945. And he too, returned to the trade his father had taught him: until his arrest in July 1963 Suchomel ran his own tailor shop in the Bavarian town of Altötting. As a passionate amateur musician and devout catholic, he also divided his spare time over no less than five orchestras and the parish church choir. His fellow Sudeten-German (and Treblinka) comrade, Gustav Münzberger, practised his catholic faith in the Bavarian town of Unterammergau, where he too continued the handicraft his father taught him: until his arrest in July 1963, Münzberger worked as furniture manufacturer. Master mason Erwin Lambert, who built the T4 gas chambers and crematoria both in Germany as well as in Poland, settled in Stuttgart after the war and set up a tile business which turned out quite successful, as his Düsseldorf judges noted in their verdict: 'In his thriving shop, he employs several tile setters.'

As a result of a traffic accident, Berlin night club waiter Franz Rum witnessed the end of the war from a hospital bed at the Timmendorfer Strand in Schleswig-Holstein, in the north of Germany. As soon as he recovered, he returned to Berlin to take up his old profession, until his retirement in 1955. And, as the final member of this group of ex-Treblinka defendants standing trial before the Düsseldorf court, there was nurse Otto Horn. His fate at the end of the war differed somewhat from that of his comrades, but he too landed safely on his feet quite soon. In late 1944 he was taken prisoner by Soviet troops near the Czech town of Ostrava and sent to a camp in Siberia. Different from most German POW's who shared his fate however, Horn was released as early as December 1946. Shortly thereafter he worked as a nurse again. In 1964 his employment with the City Hospital of Berlin was terminated by the Berlin Senate as a result of the charges brought against him.[65]

With their Sobibor and Belzec comrades things were much similar. If they survived, they simply returned home and picked up where they had left off before the war. Only very few were unfortunate enough to stumble over their murderous past and wind up in the judicial spotlights of the early post-war prosecution efforts. With most, however, their distinctive features as fieldworkers of Hitler's genocide disappeared practically overnight as they adapted themselves to the altered conditions of the new Germany.[66]

6 'Show me yourself with your dog, and I'll tell you what you are'[67]

It was certainly an awkward surprise for the successfully re-integrated T4 criminals to find that, some twenty years after their killing careers had ended, the German Federal Republic's judiciary still called them to account. As trial defendants in the dock, the aged men made a poor impression on the spectators and newspaper journalists who came to see what these thousandfold murderers looked like. Just as with the Eichmann trial of a few years earlier, it was the abyss between their personalities and their crimes which profoundly confused the audience. For here too, the discovery that 'there was nothing to discover' about these men was most shocking. Thus, the reporters who observed them in the court room recognized little else than the *Spiessbürger* (philistines) and *Biedermänner* (petty bourgeois) who, until their arrest, had been known by their neighbors as friendly, respectable and helpful citizens.[68] And while there is little doubt about the accuracy of their judgment, the fact itself only increased the exasperation over what they had once been. For it was near impossible to imagine that these 'Jekyll and Hyde' profiles could really fit the same persons.

Set off against the horrors for which these men had once been responsible, their defense appeared almost farcical. The excuses and justifications for their past conduct belonged to the rusty arsenal which had already been exhausted by their predecessors and their arguments convinced no one but themselves. Remarkable were not their many lies, distortions and 'memory losses', but the truths they inadvertently gave away about themselves and their comrades. By far the most impressive of these truths was the one showing that Hitler's extermination machinery had not been operated and staffed by an army of foam-mouthed maniacs. Contrary to what one might expect when considering the crimes these genocidal operators had committed, Sobibor, Treblinka, Belzec and the numerous other 'black holes' of the Führer's extermination project were not dependent on such representatives of the psychopathic fringe.

This does not alter the fact that among these *Aktion Reinhard* killers there were several whose former cruelties towards their victims were absolutely mind-boggling. We will not bother to recount them here in detail, as they are well-documented in their trial judgments as well as in the existing literature on the subject.[69] Paradoxically, however, of all perpetrators involved in Hitler's genocide, these so-called *Exzesstäter* ('excess perpetrators') constitute the smallest challenge to our understanding and they provided the least difficulties to their judges. It was certainly no exaggeration when the Münster anatomy professor and SS-doctor Johann Paul Kremer, spending his academic summer recess in Auschwitz in 1942, referred to his experiences as 'worse than Dante's inferno'.[70] And what applied to Auschwitz, was no less true for the rival annihilation centers of Christian Wirth. That the gatekeepers of this inferno imposed diabolical cruelties on their helpless victims is hardly the real enigma. Its opposite is. For as the statements of their surviving victims teach us, there were also camp supervisors and guards who did not engage in such 'obvious' brutalities. And yet, they too dependably and methodically performed their daily duties at the assembly line of destruction. Far more than their berserk comrades, these halfway 'considerate' mass murderers form the true question marks of the story. Undoubtedly, they were in the back of SS chief Himmler's mind when he told his SS generals on the Posen *Gruppenführertagung* of October 4, 1943 what an extraordinary achievement it was to kill thousands of people and – "apart from exceptions of human weakness" – remain "decent".[71]

So, what made these routine killers 'tick'? The obvious reference to their anti-Semitism does not help much here. Although many of them denied this afterwards, their hostile feelings towards the Jews are beyond doubt. But these feelings were not the actual reason why they murdered them. For just as in their previous, 'mercy killing' work places in Germany, they were not expected to reflect on the nature or background of those who were delivered to them in mass transports. They were hired to physically annihilate them as efficiently and as discreetly as possible. The victims themselves had already been selected and sentenced to death elsewhere and by others, such as in Berlin, by Adolf Eichmann and his likes. The only thing that was expected from the staff in the extermination camps was the implementation of these distant death sentences. Thus, theirs was the task of the executioner. And the implementation of this task did not necessarily require any 'personal inspiration' from these state-contracted killers. Above all, it required orders.

It has been said of Adolf Eichmann that his highest ambition was not so much to exterminate Jews as to follow orders. Austrian 'Nazi hunter' Simon Wiesenthal, for example, once dubbed him 'the perfect product of the system', adding that 'he would have done exactly the same if he had been given the order to kill all persons whose name began with a P or a B, or all those who had red hair.'[72] Dutch Eichmann trial reporter Harry Mulisch went a considerable step further in his characterization of the defendant:

> If, during these same years, not Adolf Hitler but Albert Schweitzer had been Reich Chancellor, and Eichmann would have received the order to transport all sick Negroes to modern hospitals, he would have carried it out without delay – with the same kind of delight in his own punctuality as with the work he completed now. He is not so much a criminal, as capable of anything.[73]

Eichmann's preparedness to assist those in need was never put to the test, but with the T4 men matters were different. After Hitler had put a stop to the gassings in August 1941, many of them were redundant. Between January and March 1942 they were temporarily put at the disposal of the *Organisation Todt* and sent to the icy front areas around Minsk and Smolensk to assist in the care of the German war wounded. After their return a new assignment awaited them: in April many of them left for the extermination camps in Poland. More than anything else, this bizarre 'humanitarian interlude' in their genocidal careers shows the crucial importance of obedience to orders in any appreciation of their conduct. In this respect we can simply multiply Mulisch's conclusion on Eichmann: they were not so much criminals as capable of anything.[74]

As far as this 'order-oriented' conditioning was concerned, these fieldworkers of Hitler's genocide showed a striking resemblance to 'Barry', the camp dog who made scores of casualties under the deportees and the 'work-Jews', in Sobibor as well as in Treblinka. Barry played a remarkably prominent role in the post-war trials against his former masters. This was already the case in the early trial against the so-called *Gasmeister* of Sobibor, Erich Bauer. By coincidence, in 1949, Bauer bumped into two camp survivors on a flea-market in Berlin. They promptly reported him with the police and, in May 1950, Bauer was tried and sentenced to death for his share in the Sobibor killings by a Berlin court.[75] Among the many accusations against him was one that involved the incitement of camp dogs against the Sobibor prisoners, including 'one, as large as a calf and a snapping St. Bernard', as it reads in the trial judgment. In the trial before the Düsseldorf court against his former comrades, fifteen years later, this 'St. Bernard' turned out to be Barry, a huge mixed breed dog, much feared among the prisoners. When left to himself, Barry was a good-natured, friendly animal who harmed nobody. When provoked by his masters, however, he turned into a snarling and biting monster. These successive masters, and particularly Treblinka's notorious deputy camp commander, Kurt Franz, used Barry to terrorize the camp inmates and the deportees along their route to the gas chambers. To Franz and his likes, it was a source of indescribably perverted fun to set up Barry against these helpless unfortunates, by shouting to him: '*Mensch, fass den Hund!*' ['Man, grab that dog!') The 'pun' here consisted of the reversal of the addressed: '*Mensch*' referred to Barry, whereas '*Hund*' stood for his victims.

In the Düsseldorf trial, Franz was among the defendants and many witnesses accused him of gruesomely maiming and killing a number of Jewish inmates with the help of Barry. The court decided to enlist the help of professionals to evaluate the stories of the witnesses. Among these experts was none other than the famous Austrian ethologist (and future Nobel Prize winner) Professor Konrad Lorenz, director of the Bavarian Max Planck Institute. Lorenz presented the court with a report that acknowledged the plausibility of the testimonies. In his view, a dog – and especially a mixed breed such as Barry – develops an infallible instinct for its master's intentions, as it 'forms the mirror image of the unconsciousness of its owner.' It could therefore very well be that, if provoked, a dog with a tender and generally friendly character would, from one moment to the next, turn into an outright monster. If the same dog subsequently changed masters again – and thus, in the words of Lorenz, developed '*eine neue Hund-Herren-Bindung*' ['a new dog-master relationship'] –, his behavior could again turn friendly overnight.

And this was exactly what had happened to Barry. When Treblinka was closed down in late November 1943, he was taken to the large military hospital in nearby Ostrow, where its chief physician became his new boss. Barry was lovingly cared after, slept under the doctor's desk and accompanied him on his daily rounds without showing any inclination to hurt any of the patients. As the doctor told the Düsseldorf judges, in 1944 he had taken Barry home to Germany and left him with his wife. Later, his brother took custody of the dog and in 1947, when Barry had weakened from old age, he was put to sleep.[76]

The psychological profile of the hybrid dog matched that of his former masters to the teeth. Prior to their recruitment for work in the extermination centers of Hitler's 'euthanasia' program, one would never have assumed that they were predestined for their careers as mass executioners, and, as we saw, after these careers had ended, they transformed into the type of civilians of whom one had not even the remotest suspicion that they could ever have been capable of such crimes. As none of the patients in the Ostrow hospital recognized in the big, good-natured dog of their doctor the ferocious animal that had, until quite recently, tore his Treblinka victims to pieces, so none of their relatives, friends or colleagues recognized the mass murderers in the T4 men who came home after the war. Thus, the director of the Ludwigsburg institute responsible for the investigation of Nazi crimes, Adalbert Rückerl, summed up their most distinctive characteristic in a succinct manner: 'Hardly any of them would have turned criminal in a society governed by the rule of law.'[77]

II Pars pro toto: Franz Stangl

> *'I have done that', says my memory. 'I cannot have done that', says my pride, and remains adamant. Finally, memory yields.*
>
> Friedrich Nietzsche, Jenseits von Gut und Böse
> [Beyond Good and Evil, translated by R.J. Hollingdale]

1 Conversations with the executioner

From Rückerl's conformists of the (un)lawful state, the West German judiciary ultimately tracked down and prosecuted some twenty-seven. The last of this group of German mass killers to stand trial was the former camp commander of Sobibor and Treblinka, Franz Stangl. Shortly before Christmas 1970 the Düsseldorf court sentenced him to life imprisonment for his leading role in the murders committed in the latter camp. The verdict would never become final, however, as Stangl died six months later, before his appeal had been decided upon.[1]

The story of Stangl's criminal career and post-war prosecution is well-suited to illustrate that of the entire group of tried *Aktion Reinhard* perpetrators as it contains nearly all ingredients common to their cases as well. Moreover, Stangl is especially interesting not only because he exceeded most of them in intelligence, but particularly also because he was by far the most communicative among them. After his conviction by the Düsseldorf court, he engaged in a series of talks with Gitta Sereny, a British investigative journalist, historian and writer of Austrian-Jewish origins. To anyone interested in 'the mind of a mass murderer', as a blurb on one of the many editions of her book would have it, Sereny's report on these talks form fascinating reading.[2] And this remains the case even when taking into account all appropriate reservations about the truthfulness of Stangl's disclosures. For one obviously needs to question his motives for consenting to the interviews at a time when the criminal case against him had not yet been decided. Sereny herself assumed that Stangl had come to his decision because he hoped to plead his case once again and find a more receptive audience among the judges of the Federal High Court of

Justice (*Bundesgerichtshof* or *BGH*), who were to decide on his appeal. She was undoubtedly right and the way the first of their talks started off only confirmed her impression. For Stangl immediately began to exhaust himself in a repetition of the defense arguments brought forward during his trial: he had never personally harmed anyone and had never wanted to hurt anyone anyhow; he had only been an insignificant subordinate who had just followed orders, and so on and so forth. It was the worn-out repertoire of all Nazi criminals before their judges, anywhere. But Sereny was far too intelligent and certainly also too interested to follow Stangl on this beaten track. Thus, she stopped him short and told him that she would only continue their discussion under strict conditions:

> I said that I knew inside out all the things he had said that morning; all of them had been said before by any number of people. And I didn't wish to argue the right or wrong of any of this; I felt it was pointless. What I had come for was something quite different: I wanted him really to talk to me; to tell me about himself as a child, a boy, a youth, a man; to tell me about his father, his mother, his friends, his wife and his children; tell me not what he did or did not do but what he loved and what he hated and what he felt about the things in his life which eventually brought him to where he was sitting now.

After some hesitation, Stangl agreed with Sereny's conditions and promised that he would try his best ('I want to do it. I want to try to do it.'). Of course, Sereny realized full well that this promise was no guarantee for Stangl's honesty, but considering the importance of the occasion it was a risk which she was willing to take:

> I thought it essential, before it became too late, to try at least once, as far as possible unemotionally and with an open mind, to penetrate the personality of a man who had been intimately involved with the most total evil our age has produced. It was important, I thought, to assess the circumstances which led up to his involvement, for once not from our point of view, but from *his*. It was a chance, I felt, to evaluate, through examining his motivations and reactions as he described them rather than as we wished or prejudged them to be, whether evil is created by circumstances or by birth, and to what extent it is determined by the individual himself, or by his environment.[3]

This was surely an ambitious agenda, but one that would turn out surprisingly worthwhile. For the answers which Stangl gave Sereny were particularly revealing, both for their contents as well as for that which they left unmentioned. And so, together with the findings of his judges, we will use them in our effort to gain further insight into the type of mass murderer to which he and his fellow trial defendants belonged.

2 'The Lord God knows me'

Next to his intelligence and willingness to talk, Stangl differed in yet another important way from his former T4 colleagues. For in contrast to them, he left Germany shortly after the war. After initially being arrested by the Austrian police and turned over to the Americans because of his SS membership, he was back in Austrian police custody in 1947. By now, the Austrian judiciary suspected him of involvement in the Hartheim killings. Before he could be put on trial, however, Stangl escaped detention in May 1948 and fled the country. First, he went to Italy, from there to Syria and finally, in 1951, to Brazil. Here, he settled with his family in São Paulo. Despite the fact that Stangl duly registered himself under his own name with the Austrian consulate, it lasted thirteen years before his whereabouts became known, due to an ordinary family row. In February 1964, Simon Wiesenthal of the Jewish Documentation Center in Vienna was tipped off on Stangl's identity and place of residence.[4] It took another three years, however, before Stangl was finally arrested and extradited to Germany to stand trial for his role as camp commander of Treblinka. Asked by a newspaper reporter on the flight to Germany about his reaction to the accusation that he had been in charge of the Treblinka killings, Stangl answered: 'I was not responsible for that which took place there.'[5] He was therefore fully confident that his case would end in acquittal. As mentioned, things went differently, however. Stangl's trial, which opened on 13 May 1970 ended seven months later with a conviction for his contribution to the murder of 'at least 400,000 persons', as it read in the verdict.

For the details of this contribution, the interested reader is referred to the judgment of the Düsseldorf court, which extensively documents Stangl's role as Treblinka's camp commander. Here, we will limit ourselves to the court's condensed characterization of the defendant and his motives. As introduction, the Düsseldorf judges cited a general conclusion which the Federal High Court of Justice had reached some eight years earlier. It dealt with the distinction between the so-called *Täter*, or principal perpetrator, and his *Gehilfe*, or accomplice. In German criminal law the difference between the two is especially important with regard to the degree of criminal responsibility awarded to the defendant, and thus to the punishment imposed. In the case of murder, the *Täter*/perpetrator automatically receives a life sentence, whereas the guilty *Gehilfe*/accomplice is eligible for a prison term between three and fifteen years. In 1962 the BGH had outlined the key features by which the perpetrator could be distinguished from the accomplice in cases dealing with 'politically inspired' crimes, such as those involving Nazi crimes:

> Whoever gives in to political incitement to murder, silences his conscience and turns criminal objectives by others into the source of his own convictions and conduct, or whoever, in his domain of duty or sphere of influence, secures that such orders are carried out unreservedly, or who shows consenting fervour in doing so, or who uses such state-organized murder terror for his own purposes, cannot argue to have been a mere accessory to his principal. His way of thinking and his actions correspond with those of the deeds' instigator. As a rule, he is a perpetrator.

According to Stangl's judges this characterization fitted their defendant to the teeth:

> He has consented to the murder of the Jews on the basis of Hitler's 'Final Solution' order and he has internalized the fundamental position of the unworthiness to live of the Jewish race. He has voluntarily accepted and fulfilled the function of camp commander of Treblinka. He has allowed his subordinates free reign in the killings and mistreatments. To him, the fate of the Jews killed in the gas chambers and the 'Lazarett' ('infirmary') was just as immaterial as that of the Jewish workers. His attitude towards the Jewish workers was determined exclusively by the importance of an undisturbed functioning of the camp system. He has willingly given in to the political incitement to the murder of the Jews, silenced his conscience and turned the criminal objectives of the instigators of the deed into the basis of his own conviction and actions. As camp commander of Treblinka he has also made sure that the criminal orders of the main perpetrators – given concrete form to him by the directives of Globocnik and Wirth – were carried out unreservedly. For his own benefit, he successfully tried, in a cautious and energetic manner, to arrange for an undisturbed operation of the extermination machinery, and to secure the appreciation of his superiors. His way of doing shows the consenting fervour, but also the concern for personal interest which the Bundesgerichtshof formulated as additional criteria for perpetrator qualification. (...)
>
> His way of thinking and his acting ... corresponded with those of the main perpetrators. In a legal sense, he is therefore to be considered equal to them and cannot appeal to having just been a mere accomplice.[6]

The verdict on Stangl could not have been more severe. Nobody who takes the trouble of reading the opinion of his judges will find any reason to disagree with them, however. Not so Stangl himself. In his closing statement he anticipated the outcome, but held out to the court: 'The Lord God knows me. My conscience does not bother me.'[7]

3 The dynamics of evil
The Austrian prologue

That Franz Stangl could not reconcile himself with the conclusion of the court is hardly a surprise. Full confessions of guilt by criminals before their judges are rare and Stangl and his previously convicted T4 comrades were again no exception to the rule. With minor variations, they all presented themselves as unwilling marionettes in a drama beyond their control; as victims of developments and superior policy decisions for which they carried no responsibility and over which they held no influence whatsoever.[8]

In the case of Franz Stangl this '*Automatik des Bösen*', or 'autonomous dynamics of evil', began after his promising career start as Austria's youngest master weaver had come to a dead end. In February 1931 he entered the Austrian urban police force. At the age of twenty-two he joined the ranks of the *Bundessicherheitswache* in Linz. During his training at the police academy Stangl and his fellow pupils were already firmly conditioned. As he recalled in his talks with Sereny, their instructors 'were a sadistic lot. They drilled the feeling in us that everyone was against us: that all men were rotten.'[9] As a rookie, Stangl was put to work as a traffic policeman but, from time to time, also assisted in the political CID.

During these years, this Austrian 'State Police' was very much occupied with investigating members of the Communist, Social-Democratic and National-Socialist parties, all of which the Dollfuss government had declared illegal. In February 1934 it came to a violent Socialist uprising in Linz which was put down by the police with considerable force. Stangl was among the policemen involved and was awarded the silver Service Medal for his role in quashing the revolt. Five months later the Austrian Nazi's launched their coup attempt, killing Chancellor Dollfuss in the process. A few days later Stangl uncovered a Nazi weapons' storage; an achievement which earned him an even more prestigious medal: the Austrian Eagle with green-white ribbon. It also opened the doors to the CID school in Linz. On July 1, 1935 Stangl was officially employed as a CID official and transferred to the office in the nearby town of Wels. In a formal capacity, he now again became involved in investigations of persons and groups associated with the political opposition against the Austrian government.

This brings us to the important question of Stangl's political orientation during the years preceding the Austrian *Anschluss* to Hitler's Third Reich, in March 1938. For what was his relationship to the illegal Austrian Nazi movement? It was a question which played a prominent role during his trial but never received a clear answer, however. According to Stangl himself, he had – before the *Anschluss* – never been a member of either the Party or the SS. As an Austrian police official he had always carried out his duty of upholding the law in an unbiased and correct manner, irrespective of whom it concerned. Among his eighteen colleagues at the Wels office there had certainly been Nazi sympathizers, but in general the Austrian police had been 'very professional', as Stangl told Sereny. Moreover, he himself had cared little for politics at the time as he had been fully occupied – apart from his work – with his young wife and new home in Wels. None the less, Stangl did admit that, on occasion, he and his colleagues had helped illegal Nazi's by providing them with information and warnings to watch their step. But this sort of assistance was equally extended to left-wing illegals (Stangl to Sereny: 'Anybody nice – decent, you know.').[10]

This self-proclaimed image of the professional and politically non-biased police official, who, every once in a while, stretched out his helping hand to 'nice persons with problems', contrasted sharply with what Stangl had written in his resume on behalf of his transfer to the Gestapo, shortly after the *Anschluss*:

> My National-Socialist attitude during the time I served in the police prompted my former teacher at the CID school, Dr. Franz Hueber, currently with the Secret Police office Salzburg, to re-instate me immediately in the service of the NSDAP after my transfer to Wels. Since this time I have also, without interruption, worked as CID official of the State Police of Wels on behalf of the intelligence service of the SS. Since I enjoyed the fullest confidence with the State Police of Wels and received all case files, I was able to prevent, or at the very least weaken, nearly all state measures which were to be taken against the National-Socialists. I hereby refer to the statement by Gauleiter Eigruber, who declared after the takeover, that the expansion of the NSDAP and its organizations in the Gau

Oberdonau, could only have been possible to this extent because of our cooperation (detectives Werner and Stangl). Additional testimonies of my illegal activities can be made by the current deputy chief of the Wels Polizeikommissariat, SS-Hauptsturmführer Herrmann Markut and by SS-Untersturmführer Dr. Bruno Wille. Also, on January 30, 1938, I was appointed SS-Oberscharführer as recognition for my contribution to the intelligence service.[11]

This pro-Nazi presentation of himself and his political background was highly incriminating in the eyes of his Düsseldorf judges as it exposed Stangl as an active advocate and pioneer of Austrian Nazism at the time that the movement was forbidden. As Austrian policeman he had thus willingly undermined the interests of the state in whose services he stood, in favor of its arch-enemies.

In reaction to this distinctly negative impression, however, Stangl came up with an alternative interpretation which blunted the sharpest edges off the story. Thus, in his trial version, the account of 1938 became a deliberate falsification of reality with the purpose of protecting him against the wrath of his new Nazi masters. For according to Stangl, the Nazi takeover in Austria, and especially the ensuing incorporation of the Wels CID bureau into the Gestapo office at Linz, had formed a direct threat to his safety. Shortly after the *Anschluss*, a number of his colleagues (who were in possession of the same Austrian Eagle medal which Stangl had earned with his anti-Nazi police work) were arrested and some of them had allegedly even been shot without further ado, while others had been sent to concentration camp. And as his personnel file clearly showed his involvement in the state's measures against pre-*Anschluss* Nazi activities, he had to fear for a similar fate. Moreover, it rapidly turned out that his relationship with his new Bavarian superior in the Linz Gestapo, Georg Prohaska, was far from amicable, and that – according to Stangl – Prohaska even threatened him with disciplinary measures.[12] With all this in mind, Stangl and his CID colleague, Ludwig Werner, had falsified their political service record with the assistance of some influential Austrian Nazi acquaintances. That his Gestapo CV showed him as an 'old fighter' for the Nazi cause was therefore no more than an attempt to save his neck, according to Stangl. And the attempt had paid off exceptionally well too, as he had been given the rank of SS-Oberscharführer and formally awarded the prestigious distinction of *alter Kämpfer*.

For obvious reasons, his judges were not much inclined to believe the story, but on the other hand they could not ignore that it carried a certain degree of plausibility. Thus, there were witnesses who appeared to support Stangl's version. First of all, there was the testimony of his former colleague, Ludwig Werner. Just as Stangl, Werner had originally belonged to the Wels CID and had been transferred to the Linz Gestapo. In October 1939, however, Gestapo chief Prohaska had Werner suspended from duty and arrested shortly thereafter, on suspicion of disloyalty to National-Socialism and of having entertained illegal contacts with a Jew. Werner was subsequently detained in the Sachsenhausen concentration camp until 1941 and then banished with his family to Bohemia, where he worked in a civil job until he was sent to the front. Between 1944 and 1948 he was in Soviet POW custody. Upon his release, he returned to Austria and to his old job with the CID, where he worked until his retirement in 1965. Three years later, Werner was questioned in connection to the case against Stangl. He could not remember all that much about his relationship with him, but in any case the two men had not been particularly close, nor could Werner recall ever having spoken about 'politics' with Stangl. Werner also claimed to be unfamiliar with any disciplinary measures the Linz Gestapo chief Prohaska might have taken or considered against Stangl, although – hardly surprising – he did confirm Prohaska's bad reputation among the Austrian CID men. Equally, Werner knew nothing about any illegal activities of Stangl on behalf of the SS or NSDAP before the *Anschluss*. In general, however, he did confirm that, out of fear for their career prospects, many Austrian police officials had retrospectively emphasized their early enthusiasm and support for the Nazi cause more strongly than reality warranted. And he also did not exclude the possibility that he had, in one way or another, been involved in Stangl's attempts to 'Nazify' his past.[13]

Stangl's explanation received an even stronger support from an unexpected source, since it was none other than the man who, as Stangl told Sereny, 'hated my guts', who confirmed important aspects of his story. In June 1970, the former Linz Gestapo chief, Georg Prohaska, now a retired CID inspector and Munich salesman, stood as a witness before the Düsseldorf court. In his testimony he left no doubt about his utter dislike for the defendant. According to Prohaska, Stangl had been known among the members of the Linz Gestapo as a '*Gesinnungslump*', an 'unprincipled swine' and an unadulterated opportunist, whose political reliability was distrusted in the highest degree: 'We had the impression of him that he would have cooperated with either side.' As Werner, Prohaska told the court that he knew nothing about any alleged pro-Nazi activities of Stangl before 1938, and he emphasized that he had always avoided contact with Stangl as much as he possibly could.[14]

Even though retaining considerable doubts, the testimonies of Werner and especially of Prohaska persuaded the Düsseldorf court to accept Stangl's version of the story. But not without putting a heavy emphasis on his opportunism. Thus, it euphemistically noted in its judgment: 'During the time of the confusing balance of power situation in Austria before 1938, the defendant chose, at the very least, not to alienate any of the political movements.' In other words: even though Stangl might not have been a Nazi by inner conviction, he certainly had been one out of convenience and calculation, according to his judges.[15]

If the court's impression was correct, Stangl's behavior was little different from that which a perceptive contemporary like the Austrian author Stefan Zweig observed about the political flexibility of his fellow countrymen. At the eve of the failed coup against the Dollfuss administration in 1934, Zweig had already witnessed the impact of the Nazi's on the Austrian civil service and the police force: 'Increasingly, I noticed from a certain insecurity in their behavior how people began to waver.' And about the mass demonstrations in support of the Schuschnigg government, shortly before the *Anschluss*, Zweig remarked,

> that most of these demonstrators only wore the required unity-badge on the collar of their overcoats for fear not to endanger their jobs, but at the same time had already registered themselves as National-Socialists in Munich, to be sure. I had learned and written too much about history not to know that the masses always immediately roll over to the side where the gravity of momentary power lies. I knew that the same throats which shouted 'Heil Schuschnigg' today, would cheer 'Heil Hitler' tomorrow.[16]

This anticipatory accommodation of citizens who snuggled up against those in power, was, of course, no exclusively Austrian trait. The Germans themselves were already years ahead of their southern neighbors in this respect. Within months after Hitler's ascend to power in January 1933, the Nazi Party was swamped by new members. In fact, the increase of membership applications became so overwhelming that the old members and the Party establishment seriously began to worry about the ideological commitment of the mass of new converts and issued a membership stop at May 1.[17] And especially also in the organization which would become chiefly responsible for carrying out Hitler's terror and extermination policies, the spectacle of police officials rapidly fine-tuning their allegiance to the new leadership was hardly exceptional, as we saw earlier in our examples of the Gestapo recruits Heinrich Müller and Franz Josef Huber. In fact, the Party bureau's skeptical appreciation of Müller's motives, cited earlier, carries a striking resemblance to Prohaska's opinion about Stangl's preparedness to serve any master to whatever purpose. With the political opportunism of which his judges suspected him, therefore, Stangl was no rare exception within the Gestapo, or even among the circle of men who were to play a pre-eminent role in the implementation of Hitler's murder projects.

And this brings us almost automatically to another crucial question about Stangl's personality. For how much of an anti-Semite was he really? Posing the question with such a hundred-thousandfold murderer as the Treblinka camp commander may appear absurd at first sight. But to anyone genuinely interested in an answer as to how and why Stangl turned into such a mega-killer, its significance should be obvious. That he himself declared never to have hated Jews does not come as a surprise. Only the opposite would have, of course, for none of the practitioners of the 'Final Solution' who stood before a judge ever claimed differently. And, wholly aside from the truth, there was at least also a very good tactical reason for such a claim. For whoever motivated his participation in these murders before his judges with the so-called base motives of racial hatred, could expect the highest punishment possible.[18] For this reason alone, even the biggest anti-Semite among them wisely refrained from disclosing such an inner persuasion.

Still, during Stangl's trial it became clear that he had at least not started out his Gestapo career as someone totally consumed by the Nazi virus of racial hatred. This was illustrated by the testimony of the former head of the Jewish community in Linz, Dr. Max Hirschfeld. Hirschfeld had a narrow escape as he managed to emigrate to the United States in December 1939. In connection to the trial against Stangl, he was heard twice, in May 1968 and again in August 1970. As he refused to come to Germany, Hirschfeld gave his testimony on both occasions in the German consulate in San Francisco.

He had met Stangl when the latter had been temporarily assigned to the *'Judenreferat'* of the Linz Gestapo. In the autumn of 1938, this 'Jewish section' was ordered by Adolf Eichmann, in his capacity as head of the Viennese Central Agency for Jewish Emigration, to assist in the forced emigration of the Jews from the former Austrian and Sudeten German areas. Hirschfeld was charged by Eichmann to register the Jews and their property. To this purpose he made two trips to the Sudetenland, accompanied by three Gestapo officials, one of whom was Stangl. As Hirschfeld recalled thirty years later, during these trips Stangl had never given him the impression that he personally harbored any hatred towards the Jews. In its trial judgment, the court summed up Hirschfeld's testimony as follows:

> The witness has described the defendant as a mere subordinate Gestapo official at the time, who always acted professionally correct and not impolite and rude towards the Jews in general, as well as also towards himself – the witness. He has also never heard that he behaved badly towards the arrested Jews. (…) Even if there could be no question of a decidedly friendly relationship between him and the defendant – as was the case according to the latter's statement – he was able to communicate with him more freely than with the other Gestapo officials. He has also heard at the time that the defendant, at the request of an aged Jewish female antique dealer named Kraus, had abstained from the arrest of her son. He could not remember, however, that in his conversations with him, the defendant had spoken about the measures against the Jews in a derogatory or disapproving manner.[19]

The impression one gets from Hirschfeld's undoubtedly reliable recollection is hardly that of the stereotyped anti-Jewish Gestapo fanatic. And so the question arises how Stangl evolved in only a short time from the polite police official who accompanied Hirschfeld, to the annihilation camp commander who found himself capable of supervising the daily killing of thousands of Jewish men, women and children. Or, to put it in the words of his judges, how he came to 'internalize the fundamental position of the unworthiness to live of the Jewish race.' The answer to this question lies in the career step Stangl took shortly after his meeting with Hirschfeld.

Hartheim and beyond

Stangl's stay with the Judenreferat lasted only two months, after which he returned to his desk at the section which dealt with the 'reactionary endeavors' of opponents to Nazi rule. Because of the continued tense relationship with Prohaska, however, he started to look around for possibilities to get away from the Linz bureau. As mentioned earlier, it was an old comrade from CID school, Franz Reichleitner, who promised him an introduction with his employer. During their talks Reichleitner allegedly did not disclose the identity of this employer nor the precise nature of the work involved, but he did mention to Stangl that it was 'a pleasant job' which concerned a 'state secret'.[20] In November 1940, Stangl was summoned to the CID head office in Berlin and received further information from a high-ranking police official by the name of Paul Werner. Werner told him that he would be assigned to the so-called Charitable Foundation for Institutional Care (the public alias of the T4 organization) to cooperate in a secret government program. Werner explained that in other parts of the world, such as in Russia and the United States, there existed laws which allowed for a mercy death for patients who suffered from mental or physical handicaps of the highest degree. Such euthanasia laws would also be introduced in Germany, but because of the sensitive nature of the issue a careful psychological preparation of the German people was required. In anticipation of formal legalization, the government had decided to secretly allow euthanasia under the strictest conditions. Thus, only patients diagnosed after careful and exhaustive medical examination as suffering hopelessly, were allowed a mercy death under this secret program. Moreover, the killing of these selected patients would be completely painless and humane, and their deaths would form a guaranteed redemption of their sufferings.

According to what he told Sereny, Stangl's initial reaction was one of perplexity and rejection. He informed Werner that he did not feel up to the task. The response was surprisingly empathetic as Werner could well understand his hesitations, but insisted that they had every confidence in his capacity to handle the assignment. Moreover, as Werner assured him, the implementation of euthanasia was exclusively in the hands of qualified doctors and nursing staff. His sole responsibility would consist of 'maintaining law and order', as Stangl expressed it in his talks with Sereny. What finally convinced him were these arguments in combination with Werner's references to his problems with Prohaska. As Werner suggested, these problems would be over if he accepted his new task. And then there was yet another argument which helped to tilt the scale: Stangl received the tempting offer to carry out his duties at only a slight distance from his family home in Wels. And so, in November 1940, he started his job as police man in the Hartheim center, near Linz.[21]

For Stangl, 'maintaining law and order' in the Hartheim extermination facility meant upholding the secrecy surrounding the killing operation as well as guarding the 'estate' of the murdered victims (including, as the court observed, their broken out gold teeth). He was also involved in the administrative processing of the killing procedure. This primarily implied monitoring the contents of the falsified death certificates, intended for the relatives of the murdered patients. Stangl remained in Hartheim until October 1941. According to the official T4 statistician, during the time of his service at the institution, 8600 patients disappeared in its gas chamber and crematorium.[22]

In late August 1941 Hitler ordered the gassings stopped as they had become too much of a public secret, causing considerable unrest among the population. This so-called euthanasia stop did not mean that the killings were terminated, however. They were now committed on an individual basis with less conspicuous methods in nursing homes scattered across the Reich. And in fact, it also did not imply the dismantling of all gas chambers. In Hartheim, for example, the chamber remained in use for the killing of concentration camp prisoners and (Eastern) forced laborers until the fall of 1944.[23] For Stangl, however, Hitler's policy change resulted in his transfer to an extermination center far from home, in Bernburg, about 45 kilometers east of the city of Marburg. Here, he was entrusted with reorganizing the chaotic administration of his predecessor, CID man Gottlieb Hering. He performed this job so well that the Berlin head office offered him the position of administrative chief, but Stangl refused. As the court echoed the defendant, 'he did not want to stay at Bernburg because of the great distance to his family in Wels.'

Shortly after his return to Hartheim he was again summoned to Berlin and told that his duties within the T4 program had come to an end. According to what Stangl told Sereny, he was offered the choice of returning to his position with the Linz Gestapo 'and put myself at the disposal of Prohaska, or, alternatively, I could elect a posting east, to Lublin.' He chose the latter, although at the time he still did not yet have any idea what this *Osteinsatz* would entail. He found out in April 1942, when he was sent to Lublin together with twenty other T4 employees. SS- and Police Leader Odilo

Globocnik and his *Aktion Reinhard* staff informed them in general terms of the task ahead and formally swore them to secrecy about their future work. Shortly thereafter they were shipped off to Sobibor, which was still in its construction phase at the time. Under supervision of an old acquaintance – former Hartheim bureau Chief Christian Wirth – Stangl and his men finished the camp. In early May Wirth tested the gas chambers with a group of Jewish workers. A few weeks later the first transports arrived and Sobibor became fully operational as a mass extermination camp under Stangl's direction.

He did not stay in Sobibor for more than a few months. In the late summer, he was transferred to Treblinka, where he became the successor of Dr. Irmfried Eberl. Eberl, former director of the T4 extermination centers at Bernburg and Brandenburg, had been Treblinka's first camp commander, but he utterly failed to cope with the organization of the mass extermination, which left the camp in chaos. When Globocnik found this out, he dismissed Eberl and had the entire camp system reorganized by Christian Wirth – by now in charge of all three *Aktion Reinhard* camps –, who picked Stangl as his assistant. As he had done in Sobibor, Stangl succeeded in turning Treblinka into a highly efficient mass extermination facility; an achievement which earned him the warm appreciation of Globocnik. In the latter's recommendation to Himmler concerning the promotion of his *Aktion Reinhard* men, Stangl was praised as 'the best camp commander, who played the largest part in the entire operation.' Himmler rewarded Stangl by promoting him to Hauptsturmführer. Stangl stayed in Treblinka until August 1943, when, together with Globocnik, Wirth and other staff members of the *Aktion Reinhard*, he left for northern Italy to perform other 'police duties'.[24]

4 Truth and fiction

It is regularly assumed that what criminals such as Franz Stangl and his comrades disclosed to the outside world about their criminal past, consisted of nothing but lies, intended to mislead their audience, first and foremost among them, obviously, their judges.[25] This general assumption calls for some differentiation, however. For certainly, their statements are filled with a great many falsehoods, denials, feigned memory losses and fabricated tales. But only the opposite would have come as a surprise, of course. It is hardly a sensational discovery that crime suspects seek to deny, or at the very least diminish, their involvement in the offences of which they stand accused. On the contrary, it belongs to the common day-to-day experience of all criminal prosecution professionals – police men, state attorneys, lawyers and judges.[26] And in this respect too, the Nazi criminals who wound up in court were again no exception.

It is certainly also true that, at times, a defense strategy based on such lies could turn out successful. Generally, this success was not so much due to the convincing nature of the lies produced, as to the absence of solid contrary evidence. And, as we shall see later on, sometimes it was even guaranteed by the disinclination of judicial authorities to properly investigate the plausibility of such a defense. In many other cases, however, the defendants' attempts to mislead the court were duly disclosed and dismantled, not least by evidence produced by the defendants themselves, or their former associates. Moreover (and contrary to yet another commonplace assumption), most of the defendants did not excel in sagacity and this was clearly noticeable in their defense arguments. As mentioned earlier, these arguments were regularly taken from the antiquated catalog employed by those who had preceded them in court, and their persuasiveness had long since ceased to impress anyone. Notable therefore, was not the fictional fabric produced by the defendants, but the truths they none the less also conveyed about themselves, their comrades and the entire modus operandi of the criminal organization which they had served. And that is why their statements matter. For they generally consisted of a mixture of truth and fiction, whereby the first often inadvertently shone through the latter. It was up to their judges to distinguish between the two by scrutinizing the plausibility of their depositions in the light of the evidence at their disposal.

Before we now turn to this issue of defense plausibility in the case of Franz Stangl and his T4 comrades, there is yet another important thing to keep in mind when considering the statements about their criminal past. For it is often overlooked that Stangl and his like were not only on trial before professional judges and an anonymous public opinion, but also faced a far more intimate audience made up of relatives, friends and colleagues. And since the opinion of this 'inner circle' affected their personal well-being at least as much as the verdict of their judges, it obviously mattered a lot to them. Moreover, next to the need to justify their past actions in court and before their family, friends and social peers, there was also the distinct psychological necessity to convince themselves, in order to maintain a degree of self-respect in an environment which considered them as the very epitome of evil. And even the harshest verdict of their judges did not affect this basic psychological need to self-confidently face both their loved ones and themselves, as we saw with Stangl's reaction to the court's conclusion: 'The Lord God knows me. My conscience does not bother me.' Whoever interprets this as a mere provocation of a cynical blasphemer misses the point. For it is precisely this psychologically compulsive claim to inner decency which explains why defendants such as Franz Stangl often exhausted themselves in the most grotesque rationalizations of their criminal conduct.

Duress of orders

There is probably no clearer illustration of the above than the persistent appeal to the so-called *Befehlsnotstand*, or duress of orders, in the post-war trials against Nazi criminals. It forms one of the most tenacious defense fictions in the history of the West German prosecution of Nazi criminals. And there are two main reasons for its popularity among trial defendants.

The first consists of the fact that duress of orders forms a legal excuse for criminal conduct under West German criminal law. Thus, the Nazi killer who could persuade his judges that he had committed his crimes on superior orders, accompanied by an otherwise unavoidable, direct threat to his own physical well-being in case of refusal, was acquitted (or discharged from prosecution) on the grounds that he could not reasonably have been expected to act otherwise. As his crimes were forced upon him 'at gunpoint', so to speak, they were, even if not legally justified, certainly excusable. This even applied if no such threat had existed in reality, but the defendant could nevertheless convince the court that he had honestly assumed that it had, and that this had been the reason for his criminal conduct. In the first instance there had existed a genuine situation of duress (*Notstand*), whereas in the second such a situation had been presumed (*Putativnotstand*).

Secondly, for Stangl and his likes the appeal to this particular line of defense remained pretty much the only means left to exonerate themselves, as their objective involvement in the mass murders was beyond doubt and was thus denied by none of them (what they denied were 'merely' the crimes they had committed on their own, personal initiatives, the so-called *Exzesstaten*).

The ideal character on whom to base the *Notstand* defense was the head of the three extermination camps, the notorious Christian Wirth. According to all who had known him, Wirth was indeed a particularly coarse and brutal personality. But above all, he was also no longer alive at the time of the trials (he had been shot dead by partisans in May 1944 near the Italian town of Trieste). And this obviously made him the favorite bogeyman in the defense of the *Aktion Reinhard* murderers.

The first who were called to form an opinion on its plausibility were the judges of the District Court of München I. In January 1964 they had to decide whether or not to try eight former German staff members of the Belzec extermination camp.[27] The court decided to drop the case against no less than seven of the accused. As the evidence in the preliminary investigations showed that they had 'only' murdered the Jews on superior orders, the judges considered this insufficient grounds to put them on trial. The reason given for this remarkable decision was that all accused had appealed to the *Befehlsnotstand*-situation, which allegedly had left them no alternative than simply to obey their killing orders. The court considered this appeal convincing because of the corresponding testimonies of the accused concerning their chief, Christian Wirth:

> Wirth, called 'Christian the Cruel' by his people, was a screaming and swearing monster, who always went through the camp carrying a whip and a pistol and who spread fear and panic wherever he appeared. He is being described by all as a National Socialist, whose ruthlessness and crudeness knew no equal and with whom, 'without intervention of an SS-court', an open refusal to obey orders would have led to certain self-destruction.[28]

And as 'self-destruction' could, of course, not be expected from anyone, the Munich judges concluded that under the circumstances Wirth's subordinates could indeed have done little else than choose the destruction of others. The State Attorney's Office appealed the decision and (among other arguments) pointed out that the only known survivor of the Belzec camp whom they had been able to trace, had testified that he had been totally unfamiliar with a 'reluctant *Einsatz* of SS-staff' in Belzec. It made no impression. On the 22 July 1964 the appeal was dismissed.[29]

There were those within the German judiciary who held a different view, however. For the casual manner with which the Munich court suspended the proceedings against the majority of the Belzec accused contrasted sharply with the almost simultaneous efforts of their Düsseldorf colleagues. Between October 1964 and September 1965 they tried ten former staff members from the Treblinka camp. The Düsseldorf court dealt at length with the question of the *Befehlsnotstand*.[30] After hearing testimonies from historical experts, former SS-judges, ex-SS-general Von dem Bach-Zelewski, a number of one-time Gestapo officials and even the retired Under-Secretary of State in the Adenauer administration, Dr. Hans Globke, and after scrutinizing a series of alleged examples of *Befehlsnotstand*, the court concluded that in reality there had not existed a general regime in which disobedience to illegitimate killing orders had resulted in excessive punishment. At worst, such disobedience had been sanctioned by demotions, transfers, forced retirement or assignment to other tasks.

In addition to this general assessment, the Düsseldorf judges scrupulously investigated the specific regime under which the defendants had served in Treblinka. As mentioned before, the central figure here was the *Aktion Reinhard* chief of operations, Christian Wirth. That Wirth had been a roughneck and an outright bully to his subordinates, who had threatened them repeatedly with severe sanctions in case of disloyalty or disobedience, was not questioned by the court. What it did question was the possibility that Wirth had ever actually had any of them shot or sent to concentration camp for refusing an order. None of the defendants or trial witnesses could produce an example of such a drastic measure or even an indication that Wirth had ever attempted anything like it. In fact, as the court concluded from the testimonies of several of them, determined opposition against Wirth's directives had, on occasion, proved successful and in any case had not met with anything more than verbal abuse or an occasional slap. Thus, the court finally concluded that for the Treblinka defendants no conditions for a *Befehlsnotstand* had actually existed.

There remained, of course, still the possibility that the defendants had nevertheless presumed otherwise at the time. As we saw, this 'putative' duress of orders could also result in acquittal if a defendant could convince the court that it had been the reason for his compliance to criminal orders. But with the exception of one, the court again denied the existence of such a *Putativnotstand* for the Treblinka defendants. That an assumed threat to their safety and well-being had not been the real motive behind their criminal conduct was obvious enough with regard to those who had engaged in excessive brutalities against their victims. Their cooperation in the killings had clearly not been prompted by dread of Wirth, but, as the court noted in its judgment, 'because Treblinka offered them the opportunity to live out their sadistic impulses, as they could murder human beings without having to fear for punishment.' But even the remaining defendants, who had abstained from such privately induced brutalities, had not really been motivated by fear of life-threatening sanctions. What had induced them to cooperate in the mass killings was 'a mistaken notion of obedience and loyalty'. And, in the courts opinion, there had also been additional reasons for their compliance, such as: 'the benefits offered to them in the camp, of which the frequent and generous vacations are to be considered the most important.'[31] Thus, the conclusion was clear:

> If an assumed danger to life and limb or an assumed exigency had really been the defendants' ... motive for cooperation in the mass killings, they would have spared no effort to escape from such an alleged constant psychological strain and be relieved from their post at Treblinka. That is not the case. For several of these defendants have undertaken nothing at all in this respect [while] others undertook too little.[32]

The possible exception referred to earlier, concerned former nurse Otto Horn, whom the court granted the full benefit of the doubt by essentially accepting his defense that he had only performed his killing duties out of fear for his life. In contrast to this co-defendants, Horn was pictured by former Treblinka inmates as an unobtrusive SS supervisor who had never mistreated any of the prisoners under his command. Allegedly, he had even been quite friendly to them, and especially to the female prisoners with whom he used to keep up 'sociable contacts' in his spare time. That Horn had genuinely disapproved of the mass killings was, moreover, confirmed by some of his co-defendants who testified that he had been scorned for his opposition to them. According to Franz Suchomel's statement, 'Horn and his friend Eisold ... had been ridiculed because they had voiced their moral reservations on the mass killings in front of their comrades and had pointed out that they could not imagine that the killing of the Jews 'would turn out well' for the Germans involved in them.'[33] As a result the two men had become shunned figures among the camp staff and Horn himself had repeatedly ran into conflict with both Wirth and T4 chief Werner Blankenburg because of his attempts to get away from Treblinka.

Even though retaining some doubts in this respect, the Düsseldorf judges acquitted Horn due to 'insufficiently certain proof of his guilt'. After reviewing the evidence in his case, they considered it 'probable' that Horn had indeed only carried out his murderous duties out of fear for severe punishment in case of disobedience. At the same time the court stressed that there could be no question of an acquittal 'because of proven innocence', since the exculpatory evidence in his case had not been unambiguously established.[34]

Three days before the Düsseldorf court reached its verdict, a third trial opened before the Hagen court which addressed the *Aktion Reinhard* murders. This time it concerned twelve former staff members of the Sobibor annihilation camp. As their Düsseldorf colleagues, the presiding judges showed themselves equally unimpressed by the ease with which the Munich court had earlier dismissed its accused in the Belzec case. In fact so much so that out of the seven men whom 'Munich' had sent home without a trial, five were now recalled to the dock to answer for their role in the Sobibor murders. Essentially, the findings of the Hagen judges with regard to the *Befehlsnotstand* question were similar to those of their Düsseldorf colleagues. In the end, however, they still felt obliged to acquit five of the defendants on the grounds of *Putativnotstand*.[35]

The findings of the Düsseldorf and Hagen judges with regard to the *Befehlsnotstand* defense were confirmed in many other trial cases related to the regime's extermination policies. Over time, court officials, defense counsel, historians and – last but not least – organizations of former SS members tried to discover solid evidence to demonstrate that a life-threatening situation had in fact existed for those ordered to carry out the extermination measures. But despite repeated claims to this effect, not one single case could be produced which stood up under scrutiny. This led to the obvious conclusion that the *Befehlsnotstand* argument had indeed no basis in reality. For there could be no doubt that if such a coercive regime had existed within Hitler's genocidal universe, it would have been common knowledge to all involved, and would certainly have enabled them to produce the evidence required to convince the courts without any difficulty. That they were unable to do so, was quite simply because there was nothing to find. A telling comment in this respect came from Werner Best, former high-ranking official of the Reichssicherheitshauptamt and post-war 'expert' trial witness on the subject:

> After I had experienced no case of punishment because of a refusal to an order during the war myself, I made an effort after the war — as I tried to assist old comrades in my 'practice on the side' – to establish such cases for use in the ongoing criminal proceedings. Despite questioning numerous 'competent' men – particularly judges of the SS and the Wehrmacht – I was unable to establish even a single suitable case.
>
> I subsequently turned the tables and, in my depositions concerning the Befehlsnotstand, I stressed the observation that, in my view, cases of punishment for refusals to orders had not come to my attention because at the time we had all been convinced that insubordination was impossible, and that therefore such cases had hardly or not occurred.[36]

For a lawyer out to help his former comrades with their court defense this was certainly a cunning solution, especially as it carefully ignored the alternative possibility: namely, that cases of disobedience were absent simply because no one had ever actually bothered about the justifiability of the killing orders.

As the courts convincingly demonstrated, however, the notion that Hitler's genocidal fieldworkers had been forced to conduct their murderous duties under pressure of life-threatening sanctions, turned out fictitious. And in most cases this also applied to the idea that the killers had (wrongly) assumed differently. The motives for their criminal conduct clearly lay elsewhere, and in the case of the *Aktion Reinhard* accomplices, the Düsseldorf and Hagen judges identified them as related to the privileged and relatively comfortable existence these men enjoyed in the annihilation camps.[37] This was no different for Franz Stangl. Even though his judges were willing to accept his claim that he had considered the killings an 'outrage' (*'eine Ungeheuerlichkeit'*), they unhesitatingly dismissed his appeal to the effect that he had been forced to supervise them. This, as the court noted, was no more than an obvious attempt to justify his behavior (*'eine blosse Schutzbehauptung'*). What had prompted him to his actions had been neither the fearful reputation of his chief, Christian Wirth, nor, for that matter, any deep ideological conviction or profound hatred of his victims, but the two character traits that ran 'like a red thread' through his entire career: blind ambition and opportunism.[38]

As emphasized earlier, for trial defendants such as Stangl, the *Befehlsnotstand* argument was, however, far more than a mere defense strategy. For to have this argument swept aside by their judges was one thing, but to have to admit to their wives and children, and – ultimately – also to themselves, that they had committed their unimaginable crimes out of purely self-centered, opportunistic motives, was an outright psychological impossibility. That is an additional reason why, with exasperating tenacity and against all odds, they continued to clutch at the fable that they had been forced to their deeds and could have acted no differently than they had. Indeed, such retrospective rationalizations of their behavior formed little else than a psychological necessity for these men, which explains why they belonged to the standard repertoire of all of them, including Franz Stangl.

The incorruptible policeman: Stangl's self-portrait

Even though he was in charge of all aspects concerning the smooth operation of the extermination procedures at Treblinka, Stangl kept his distance from its daily practice, which he generally left in the hands of his deputy, the notorious Kurt Franz. He himself mainly 'limited' his involvement to administrative and supervisory tasks. But even though leaving the actual 'processing' of the transports to others, he did regularly witness them, standing on the high earthen wall that ran through the camp, like 'a lord of the castle', as a former inmate put it in his testimony.[39] To everyone in the camp – T4 men, Ukrainian or Lithuanian guards, Jewish workers –, as well as to Globocnik's *Aktion Reinhard* staff, Stangl was the undisputed commander of Treblinka however. And as he had been the highest in rank (police lieutenant) among the camp's German staff, even he himself admitted to having been in charge.

During his trial and in his talks with Sereny, Stangl nevertheless maintained that he had not been camp commander, either in Sobibor or in Treblinka, on the grounds that he had never been formally appointed as such. That this made no difference whatsoever as far as the appreciation of his role was concerned, hardly seemed to have dawned on him. This remarkable and 'denialist' proneness to formalities was typical of Stangl's disclosures about his past and forms a clear illustration of his desperate efforts to uphold a decent self-image in view of the charges brought against him. This becomes particularly clear in three anecdotes which Stangl voluntarily presented in his interviews with Sereny.

The first concerned his function as police official in the Hartheim extermination center. As mentioned before, Stangl was never tried for his involvement in the Hartheim murders and they only played a marginal role in the Treblinka trial. But in his talks with Sereny he told her a story about his Hartheim experiences which illustrates the above in a telling fashion. Asked by her how he had felt at the time about the justifiability of what went on at Hartheim, Stangl answered by telling her of a complaint which he had received one day. It concerned a mother whose child had been killed at the center. According to regular procedure, the mother had been sent the personal belongings of the child, together with its falsified death certificate. The mother complained, however, that she missed a candle (!), which she had given the child shortly before it had been secretly transferred from the nursing home where she had lived. In order to find out what had happened to the candle, Stangl visited the nursing home, which was run by nuns. He was received by the Mother Superior, who showed him a severely handicapped boy 'lying in a basket'. The boy appeared five years old, but was in fact – according to the nun – sixteen and hopelessly underdeveloped. To her great dismay (and that of the priest who was also present) the T4 Doctors' Committee who had earlier visited the institution, had refused to include the boy among the patients selected for killing. Stangl's comment to Sereny: 'This really shook me. Here was a Catholic nun, a Mother Superior, and a priest. And they thought it was right. Who was I then, to doubt what was being done?'[40]

Of course, it is impossible to check the authenticity of this bizarre story. But that is of no importance here. What matters are the two reasons why Stangl told it to Sereny. The first is plain enough: Stangl told it in an attempt to justify his cooperation in the 'mercy killing' program by placing the moral responsibility on the shoulders of two such distinguished representatives of the Catholic Church as the nun and the priest. If they supported the government's medical killing program, how then could he, as a simple policeman, doubt its justifiability? The answer to this rhetorical question should – in Stangl's eyes – be obvious: it could not have been expected from him under these circumstances. Clearly, one might dismiss this argumentation as morally unacceptable, but in itself it still remains intelligible.

This is not the case with the second reason behind Stangl's story. For it consists of Stangl's outrageous attempt to present himself as the duty-bound and incorruptible police officer who resisted injustice under all circumstances, i.e. even within the environment of mass murder. What he obviously failed to appreciate was that, with this overwrought effort, he pronounced a devastating comment on himself. For the totally ridiculous and trivial motive (the 'missing candle') he presented as cause for his 'investigation' merely underlined the bizarre mind-set of the mass murdering bureaucrat appealing to his professional ethics. And it is indeed hard to think of a more damning self-image than this.

That it was definitely no 'slip of the tongue' was shown even more clearly in the other two examples Stangl presented to Sereny. The first concerned an incident which occurred shortly after the arrival of a deportation transport in Treblinka. One of the Jews from this transport approached Stangl and said that he wanted to make a complaint: 'So I said yes, certainly, what was it.' The man thereupon told him that one of the Lithuanian guards had promised him some water in exchange for his watch. He had handed the guard his watch, but had received no water from him in return. Stangl promptly reacted: 'Well, that wasn't right, was it? Anyway, I didn't permit pilfering. I asked the Lithuanians then and there who it was who had taken the watch, but nobody came forward.'

His deputy, Kurt Franz, warned Stangl that it could have been one of the Lithuanian officers and that he could hardly embarrass an officer in front of his men. Again, Stangl reacted immediately: 'Well, I said, "I am not interested what sort of uniform a man wears. I am only interested in what is inside a man."' Allegedly, he then ordered the guards to line up and empty their pockets. At this point, Sereny interrupted him and asked if all this took place in front of the prisoners? Stangl's answer: 'Yes, what else? Once a complaint is made it has to be investigated. Of course we didn't find the watch – whoever it was had got rid of it.' When Sereny thereupon inquired after the fate of the complainant, Stangl showed himself surprised at the question and briskly answered that he had no idea. It was obvious that he had never given this question a moment's thought.[41]

Again, whether or not this horrifying anecdote had any basis in reality is of no significance here. But, as with the first story, it underlines Stangl's obsession to impress his interlocutor with his 'righteousness', even under the most absurd conditions.

Although hardly imaginable, Stangl succeeded in surpassing even this example of his failure to grasp the true nature of his account. For the third story the told Sereny was even more spine-chilling. It involved his contacts with the so-called *Arbeitsjuden* [work Jews] in Treblinka. Stangl described these contacts as 'friendly' and pleasant: 'Beyond my specific assignment, that's what I enjoyed; human relations.' He entertained such relations above all with two Austrian Jews ('after all, I *was* Austrian.'), which he gave preferential treatment. One of them was a Viennese Jew, named Blau, who asked Stangl for a favor:

> There was one day when he knocked at the door of my office about mid-morning and stood to attention and asked permission to speak to me. He looked very worried. I said, 'Of course, Blau, come on in. What's worrying you?' He said it was his eighty-year-old father; he'd arrived on that morning's transport. Was there anything I could do. I said, 'Really, Blau, you must understand, it's impossible. A man of eighty....' He said quickly that yes, he understood, of course. But could he ask me for permission to take his father to the *Lazarett* rather than the gas chambers. And could he take his father first to the kitchen and give him a meal. I said, 'You go and do what you think best, Blau. Officially I don't know anything, but unofficially you can tell the Kapo I said it was all right.' In the afternoon, when I came back to my office, he was waiting for me. He had tears in his eyes. He stood to attention and said, 'Herr Hauptsturmführer, I want to thank you. I gave my father a meal. And I've just taken him to the *Lazarett* – it's all over. Thank you very much.' I said, 'Well, Blau, there's no need to thank me, but of course if you want to thank me, you may.'[42]

It was at this point that Sereny nearly broke off her talks as she considered herself no longer able to cope with Stangl's profound lack of empathy with the victims in his story. That she finally decided to continue had to do with her certain conviction that Stangl was about to disclose an important truth about himself. Below, we will return to this 'revelation'.

The awareness of injustice

When reading Stangl's story, one easily imagines Sereny's desperation over its exasperating callousness and absence of any appreciation of its horror. Indeed, one is tempted to conclude that it could only have been the tale of a depraved person. But the problem is that Stangl wasn't, nor were most of his fellow T4 men. This prompts one of the most pressing questions about the state-employed mass murderers of the likes of Stangl: while conducting their murderous duties in Sobibor, Belzec, Treblinka or elsewhere, did they have any qualms whatsoever about the sufferings they inflicted upon their victims? Or, to put it more generally: to what extent did they recognize the injustice of their acts at the time of their committal? The answer to this question is crucial not only for our perspective on the psychology of these men, but more specifically also for the professional opinion of their judges on the measure of their guilt. As has been argued earlier, the establishment of subjective guilt presupposes a sense of wrong-doing, an awareness of injustice. Wherever the latter is absent, the former must fail.

For this reason, the question of the awareness of injustice, or '*Unrechtsbewusstsein*', played a central role in the West German trials of Hitler's executioners. Remarkably enough, nearly all of them admitted having had this sense of wrong-doing at the time and therefore of having realized the criminal nature of the killings they were ordered to carry out. Because of these voluntary confessions but also because of the apparent nature of the injustice itself, the courts generally assumed that such an awareness had indeed been present among these men. Thus, as we saw earlier, the Düsseldorf judges accepted Stangl's recognition that he had considered the mass murder of the Jews as a profoundly criminal 'outrage'. And their Hagen colleagues noted in their judgment that, considering the circumstances in Sobibor, even the most simple-minded ('*auch der Primitivste*') could not have escaped the horrifying injustice committed there.[43]

Viewed from a criminological perspective, however, such conclusions about the qualms of conscience with Stangl and his men are not always as convincing as they might seem. On the one hand, this has to do with the indissoluble link between the awareness of injustice on the one hand, and the defense of duress on the other. After all, the acknowledgment of the first forms the precondition for the second: without recognizing the unlawful and unjust nature of the murderous tasks they had been assigned, the argument that they had been compelled to carry them out against their will obviously made no sense. And so, Stangl's effusion before his judges about the outrageousness of his extermination duties was at least also given in by his appeal to the *Befehlsnotstand*; an appeal which, as we saw, the court dismissed as an all too recognizable attempt to exculpate himself. What this means is that Stangl's alleged abhorrence of the killings might have been genuine, but it certainly also allows for a considerably more cynical interpretation.

Secondly, the conclusion that the criminal nature of the things practised in the extermination camps on a daily basis should have been obvious to all participants, is not as self-evident as it might appear. For this obviousness can certainly not be inferred automatically from the conduct of the defendants at the time. A highly dramatic illustration of this concerned the performance of former dairy master Willi Mentz in Treblinka. As his co-defendants, Mentz admitted in court that he too had recognized the criminal nature of the killings he engaged in. But during his regular duties at the execution pits of the *Lazarett* (where – as the court established on his own admissions – he personally shot thousands (!) of men, women and children), Mentz displayed a degree of cold-heartedness which bordered on the unimaginable and in fact showed a complete lack of any such sense of wrong-doing. On the other hand, the court also noted that, while performing other (non-killing) duties in Treblinka, Mentz's behavior was of a totally different character:

> He did not beat the prisoners of the farming work force entrusted to him, as he felt no inclination to it and because he was not ordered to. As he himself put it, decisive for him was the motto '*Befehl ist Befehl*', whereby it was indifferent to him whether he was employed in a peaceful activity such as farming or as the executioner of innocent people.[44]

This 'Jekyll-and-Hyde' type of performance prompted the court to dub Mentz's behavior as that of 'a soulless robot', and it is indeed highly doubtful whether he experienced any emotion at all while carrying out his duties. None the less, and as it did with his co-defendants, the court found that Mentz too had indeed recognized the distinctly criminal nature of his acts at the time he committed them. And, short of acquitting him for gross mental deficiency – which clearly didn't apply to him –, the court had in fact no other option as criminal law doctrine requires an awareness of injustice as precondition for the establishment of guilt. In criminal law there is no room for 'soulless robots' as they obviously cannot be held accountable for their actions. Thus, from a legal point of view even the robot has to be 'equipped' with awareness of injustice in order to assess his criminal responsibility and pronounce a substantiated judgment on his actions. What this means is that with defendants such as Willi Mentz, the courts had to assume the existence of an active conscience which, however, remains dubious from a strictly factual point of view.[45]

But if the true nature of their feelings at the time remains difficult enough to reconstruct, how about these feelings when they faced their judges, decades later and under radically different social and political circumstances? Looking back on what they had done, was there at least some appreciation of its injustice or the slightest twinge of remorse? As strategic, defense-related considerations and the maintenance of a respectable self-image on the part of these defendants obscure the answers to these questions, it again remains difficult to say. That Hitler's mass extermination program constituted a crime of the profoundest proportions was no longer denied by any of them, but the sincere acknowledgment of a personal responsibility for their participation in it was something that most eschewed from. Whereas none went so far as Stangl's former adjutant and notorious killer, Kurt Franz, who prided himself in court as 'savior' of the Jews, most still regarded themselves as helpless pawns at the mercy of omnipotent superior forces.[46] And, of course, it would again be naïve to expect otherwise. For the sincere recognition of their role in the unimaginable horrors of Hitler's mass murderous project collided head-on with both their defense tactics as well as with huge personal psychological barriers. These barriers could only be lifted at a price which would destroy the final vestiges of self-respect. And with few exceptions, this was a price they could not possibly bring themselves to pay.

If we may believe Sereny, however, Franz Stangl may have been the exception to this rule. He died of a heart attack one day after finishing his talks with her with something she took as a hesitantly and clumsily expressed, but none the less genuine recognition of his personal guilt: 'So yes, in reality I share the guilt.... Because my guilt ... my guilt ... only now in these talks ... now that I have talked about it all for the first time....'[47] And even though Sereny was well aware that Stangl suffered from a severe heart condition from which he probably would have died soon anyhow, she was convinced that there was a causal relationship between these final words and his sudden death: 'I think he died when he did because he had finally, however briefly, faced himself and told the truth; it was a monumental effort to reach that fleeting moment when he became the man he should have been.'⁴⁸

Certainly, one could dismiss her conclusion as wishful thinking as there is, after all, nothing more reassuring than the idea that even a mass murderer such as Franz Stangl is ultimately capable of sincere self-reflection (*and* pays the price for it). On the other hand, it is not impossible that his defense mechanisms and retrospective rationalizations exhausted themselves in the course of their conversations up to the point where they finally lost all persuasiveness even to Stangl himself. Whoever reads Sereny's report on these talks will find that he certainly did not lack the necessary intelligence for this. Moreover, one gets the impression that, after a while, Stangl indeed genuinely tried to do what he promised at the outset, namely to answer Sereny's questions as honestly as he could. If true, Stangl's death formed a clear answer to the pressing question which one of his young prison guards put to Sereny, just prior to the beginning of her interviews:

> Perhaps now at long last one of them is going to have the courage to explain to my generation how any human being with mind and heart and brain could … not even 'do' what was done – it isn't our function to say whether a man is 'guilty as charged' or not – but even see it being done, and consent to remain alive.⁴⁹

III The Palmström Syndrome

> *It obviously belongs to the human mechanisms for self-preservation, that we simply cannot or will not imagine a person playing a significant role in decisions about our fate, as a paltry figure. Whoever experiences sorrow, humiliation and loss does not also wants to be the victim of pure mediocrity, because the idea that a zero holds power over us is even more unbearable than that someone holds power over us. This mechanism in turn distorts a clear view of the perpetrator.*
>
> Bettina Stangneth, *Eichmann vor Jerusalem.*

1 A magical encounter

To the historian, it remains a tantalizing fantasy: the thought that Sigmund Freud and Adolf Hitler might have stumbled into each other on their daily strolls through the center of the Austrian capital. And it is not even such an unlikely idea, for during his Viennese years – roughly between 1907 and 1913 – Hitler, as he wrote in *Mein Kampf*, 'from the early morning until late at night', wandered around the same part of the city which Freud used to traverse on his daily walks from his home at the Berggasse 19. Thus, for example, on the most famous street of Vienna: 'For hours I could stand in … front of the Opera, for hours admire the Parliament; the entire Ringstrasse worked on me like magic from One Thousand and One Nights.'[1] And the churches which the young artist portrayed – the *Minoriten-*, *Votiv-*, *Karls-* and *Peterskirche* – were all within short walking distance from Freud's home. So the idea that, one day, the two men may have passed each other within just a few yards, or even that they were inadvertently captured together in a picture taken by one of the many Viennese street photographers – an idea by George Steiner – is certainly not all that far-fetched.[2] We will not over-strain the imagination by speculating that they may even have exchanged a few words on the occasion, but from a historical point of view it would in any case have been a highly dramatic spatial encounter between the Jewish intellectual giant and the 'absolute anti-Semite', as Hitler identified himself in his testimony before the Munich court some years later. And it would definitely also have been a meeting between two Viennese residents who, as none other, would leave their indissoluble marks on twentieth century Western civilization.

It is hard to imagine two worlds further apart: the one of the erudite humanistic scholar and architect of psychoanalysis and that of the poorly educated, racist megalomaniac and initiator of the largest bureaucratic mass murder Europe ever witnessed. And yet, both Freud's and Hitler's legacy share something of importance. Thus, whatever one may hold of Freud and his theories, few would probably question the appreciation of one of his pupils:

> What was epoch-making in Freud's findings was that he found the key to the understanding of the system of forces which make up man's character system and to the contradictions within the system. The discovery of unconscious processes and of the dynamic concept of character were radical because they went to the roots of human behaviour; they were disquieting because nobody can hide any longer behind his good intentions; they were dangerous, because if everybody *were* to know what he *could* know about himself and others, society would be shaken to its very foundations.

As a set of theories of human personality, psychoanalysis was thus potentially highly 'explosive', which appears to be the reason why its 'detonator' was removed. In popularized and ridiculed form Freud's ideas on the all-encompassing importance of sexual instincts found their way to general recognition. Filtered out were the more disturbing aspects of his theories:

> To discover repressed character traits such as narcissism, sadism, omnipotence, submission, alienation, indifference, the unconscious betrayal of one's integrity, the illusory nature of one's concept of reality, to discover all this in oneself, in the social fabric, in the leaders one follows – this indeed is 'social dynamite.'[3]

Freud died in his London exile in the very month Hitler's troops invaded Poland and ignited the Second World War. Thus, he was spared the spectacle from which he would probably have recoiled even in his gloomiest conjectures about humanity.[4] But in many ways, that which took place behind the German front lines within the following six years formed the radical confirmation of his ideas. For the irrational image of man which constituted the very nucleus of these ideas found its most gruesome expression in Hitler's genocidal universe. And in this respect Hitler's legacy shows a striking kinship to Freud's. As the psychoanalyst had theoretically stripped man's image of himself of the final vestiges of decency, integrity and rationality, it was Hitler's 'merit' to put this naked image of man on display on the stages of Auschwitz and the innumerable other platforms of his extermination frenzy. As none other before him, Hitler demonstrated just how breathtakingly easy it was to turn the decent, respectable and rational twentieth century German and Austrian middle-class citizen into a mass murderer of defenseless men, women and children. Ultimately, all it took turned out to be an appeal to his self-interest; an appeal which melted away his decent, respectable and rational qualities like snow before the sun. Once required of him, the unobtrusive and obedient subject of Hitler's empire of injustice effortlessly adopted a killer role. And if he was given the opportunity, he returned to his old status as family man and respected member of civil society the moment this empire had gone up in smoke and the rule of justice had once again been restored. The psychology of this 'bourgeois somersault' is unmistakably Freudian and displays the full and dazzling spectrum of rationalization, defense and repression mechanisms which the human intellect is capable of mobilizing when it finds cause to do so.

Each in his own way then, both Freud and Hitler showed what the 'emperor's clothes' were made of and how feeble the façade of civil respectability really was. And, not least, they also showed the world behind this façade. It was a panorama which was devastating for the average middle class citizen's self-esteem. To find out that he was by no means the reasonable and balanced personality which he presented of himself, but a servile follower of primitive motives and mundane instincts which respected no other interests than his own, was clearly too much of an affront to his self-respect. Thus, the message called for drastic mutilation. This applied to that of Freud, but particularly also to that of Hitler. After 1945, his criminal legacy was therefore rapidly reduced to the lesson which spelled out the horrifying consequences of racial hatred and anti-Semitism. Paradoxically, this was a comforting and relatively innocent lesson to which all now agreed as – except for the small group of condemnable killers –, none had allegedly ever harbored such sentiments. And with the general acceptance of this lesson, the sting of the message was silently removed. For conveniently ignored, of course, was the question whether there were not perhaps also additional reasons and explanations for the recent European catastrophe; reasons and explanations that called for a profound self-critical reflection on the ostensibly respectable and balanced reputation of modern society. More particularly also, explanations which sought the answer to the Nazi horrors not exclusively in a mysterious popular outburst of racial hatred and xenophobia, but in the adverse qualities of a common pattern of 'civil' behavior.

2 The criminal of the century

In the very same month in which the Red Army liberated Auschwitz, Hannah Arendt would put her finger on this sore spot in an article in the American journal *Jewish Frontier*. Referring to French author Charles Péguy, who had dubbed the common man 'the great adventurer of the twentieth century', Arendt noted that he had also turned out to be 'the criminal of the century': 'Himmler's over-all organization, relies not on fanatics, nor on congenital murderers, nor on sadists; it relies entirely upon the normality of jobholders and family-men.'[5] With mixed feelings, Arendt would set eyes on the accuracy of her views some fifteen years later in the Jerusalem court room. And this accuracy would be confirmed over and over again in the subsequent German trials against the collaborators of Hitler's extermination agenda. As in the Jerusalem case, the baffling discrepancy between the crimes committed and the criminals in the court benches could no longer escape anyone. Typical in this respect was the comment of a Hamburg judge, presiding over a case involving the mass killings in the Warsaw ghetto and the Treblinka extermination camp:

> One looks for ... the great criminal and encounters careerism, zeal, subalternity, submissive eagerness, intellectual and moral thoughtlessness, blind trust in the leadership and a complete abandonment of the self and its responsibilities.[6]

What the Hamburg judge somewhat despairingly expressed here, was that, in the character traits which had prompted his defendants to 'follow Hitler on his murderous path', he discovered a striking resemblance with behavior characteristics from everyday life.

For those who have difficulty with such a conclusion, it might be helpful to take a step back and cast a brief sideward glance at calamities which occur in normal societies governed by the rule of law. Take, for example, the financial crisis which hit global economies a few years ago with such devastating effects. In its aftermath, extensive investigations and parliamentary inquests were set up to discover its root causes and identify its culprits. Invariably, the reports resulting from these in-depth examinations did not so much expose arch-villains and criminals out to undermine or dismantle the financial and socio-economic system, but its formerly celebrated representatives: bankers and financial experts who lured their clients into accepting dubious and obscure transactions and constructions. They consisted of blind careerists, status seekers, bonus traders, profit hunters and failing supervisors. Prompted by perverse incentives, they unscrupulously sought to maximize the yield for both their shareholders and themselves, without taking any notice of the general consequences of their actions for society as a whole, or indeed of their personal responsibilities for them.[7]

Some highly illustrating examples of this disposition and the environment from which it springs, can be found in the book by Dutch journalist and writer Joris Luyendijk on the morals within the international banking community.[8] In Luyendijk's vivid account of his talks with the financial wizards of the London City, he illuminates the absent morality within this monetary 'meritocracy'. Such as illustrated, for example, by the former member of this financial caste who gave up his banking career after ten years and recalled his past from a 'Faustian' perspective:

> You sell your soul to the devil. I sold my soul for worldly riches. The price the devil demanded was my moral bankruptcy. For a long time I was OK with that, until I wasn't. What triggered this change of heart? There was not one particular moment. You have to look yourself in the mirror every morning. I imagined a future son or daughter asking me, Daddy, what do you do for a living? What was I going to say? "Well, sweetie, Daddy rips clients off?"

Another striking observation in this respect is that which Luyendijk received from the man who facilitated the careers of these bankers with his recruitment agency: 'My clients are not bad people. They are people who no longer think in terms of good and evil. *Professionals.*' Seen in the light of the catastrophic consequences of their actions such a comment is undoubtedly shocking. But, as Luyendijk also makes clear, one could make no bigger mistake than to interpret this 'professional mind-set' as the mere outcome of a private immorality. Above all, it was (and is) the result of an environment which these 'professionals' represented; an environment in which – as one of Luyendijk's other informers expressed it – the ultimate character test is 'if you can say no to earning three, four or five times your current salary?'[9]

The upright reader will quite probably protest here and argue that the environment of the dubious financial adventurer is worlds apart from that of 'Wannsee', and that one cannot possibly compare his recklessness and callous manipulations with the planned physical annihilation of human beings. And, of course, such an objection would be in place. Except for one important aspect, however. For the egoistic impulses of the financial traders and bankers, whipped to unprecedented heights by an uncontrolled neo-liberalism on the one hand, and those of the genocidal collaborators, employed in the service of a criminal regime on the other, were very much alike in their shared (im)material self-interest. To the first, this self-interest expressed itself in exuberant financial rewards and corresponding social status; to the second, in the uniquely privileged position of Hitler's '*Geheimnisträger im Sondereinsatz*' ('bearers of secrets on special assignment'). The rewards connected to this latter position prompted the Düsseldorf court in its judgment on one of them – gas chamber builder Erwin Lambert – to make a telling observation: 'Under these circumstances it is not surprising that he liked his three assignments in Treblinka, and that he undertook nothing to be relieved of them.'[10]

Of course, this egocentric mind-set was not limited to the genocidal fieldworkers at the end of the line of command to which Lambert and his like belonged. From the top down, the entire Nazi apparatus was saturated with it. As crown witness one could call Hitler's most prominent 'professional', his Minister of Armaments, Albert Speer. In the voluminous report of her long-lasting efforts to analyze Speer's 'battle with truth', Gitta Sereny describes a confrontation with him over his enduring denial of having known Hitler's extermination agenda. Asked after his reaction if he *had* been aware of it, Speer answered as follows:

> Don't you know that this is the question I have asked myself a million times, continuously hoping that I would be able to give myself an answer I could live with? ... My answer to myself is always the same.... I would somehow have gone on trying to help that man win his war.[11]

Whether this was indeed the answer which Speer found that he 'could live with' remains an open question, but his recognition of unconditional loyalty to Hitler does show a certain courageous honesty. For with it, Speer exposed a side of his personality which hardly spoke in his favor. Sereny interpreted his unrestrained devotion to Hitler as the result of the special emotional chemistry which is said to have existed between the two men; a bond which Speer himself characterized as that between Faust and Mephisto. But there was at least also a distinctly less literary side to Speer's *Führertreue*. He had made this quite clear earlier on in his memoires, when he wrote how his friend, Gauleiter Karl Hanke, had urged him never to visit a concentration camp in Upper-Silesia (Auschwitz), where he – Hanke – had witnessed things he dared not talk about: 'I didn't enquire with him, I didn't enquire with Himmler, I didn't enquire with Hitler, I didn't talk to personal friends. I investigated nothing – I didn't want to know what went on there.'[12]

According to Speer, it was a 'deliberate blindness' for which he had a very good reason: 'Because out of fear to discover something which could have prompted me to face the consequences, I closed my eyes.'[13] It is of some significance that Speer – who was obviously very anxious to choose the right words for this key passage in his memoirs – used the auxiliary verb '*could*' in this connection instead of the far more compelling '*should*'.[14] For it seems to express a reservation which confirms what he was to tell Sereny years later, namely that he would have remained loyal to Hitler even with full knowledge of what was being done to the Jews. And the reason for this was not merely rooted in the Mephistophelian bond between the two men, or in Speer's fear for possible life-threatening sanctions in case he distanced himself from Hitler. Above all, it was given in by the other, quite pragmatic side of the 'consequences' to which Speer referred here: the inevitable loss of a position of power unequaled by that of any other of the Führer's leading associates. Put differently: Speer was simply not prepared to give up his top position at the Olympus of the Third Reich, the Obersalzberg, even for Auschwitz.[15] More than anything else then, it was Speer's concern over his career perspectives which made him fear to discover something that 'could' cause him to act.

Speer's self-chosen blindness was no different from that of Hitler's more experienced genocidal collaborators who wound up in court. As the armament's minister, they emphatically denied having known of the fate of those whom they persecuted and deported to their deaths. Take Karl Wolff, for example, right-hand man of Heinrich Himmler.[16] Together with his SS chief, Wolff witnessed a mass shooting of Jews in Minsk in August 1941, and, one year later, secured the necessary transport facilities which allowed for the deportation of the 300,000 remaining Jews from the Warsaw ghetto to the extermination camp of Treblinka. In a personal thank-you note to the man who had provided the trains – Under-Secretary of State at the Reich Transport Ministry Albert Ganzenmüller – Wolff wrote: 'With particular pleasure I noted from your message that, since 14 days now, daily trains with each 5000 members of the chosen people are running to Treblinka, and that we are accordingly still in the position to continue with this population movement at an accelerated pace.'[17] Standing before his judges in September 1964, however, Wolff maintained only to have heard of Hitler's extermination plans at the end of the war.

Franz Rademacher, head of the 'Jewish department' in the German Foreign Office and in this capacity involved in the order to shoot detained Serbian Jews and deport Serbian, Croatian, Rumanian, German, French, Belgian and Dutch Jews to Poland and prevent their emigration to Palestine, had also been unaware of the murderous agenda of his superiors. As his Nuremberg judges noted in their judgment of March 1952: 'The defendant denies knowledge of the extermination plan.'[18] Rademacher's colleague in the 'Jewish department', Fritz-Gebhardt von Hahn, instrumental in the deportation of Jews from Thrace and Macedonia to Auschwitz and Treblinka, likewise had no idea what he had been doing:

> At the time, he knew nothing about the fate of the deported Jews. He assumed that the Jews – in part for security reasons – were taken elsewhere and that the evacuation was undertaken with the purpose of employment in the East. He only had a general idea of this; no knowledge of details whatsoever.[19]

Hellmuth Reinhard, head of the Gestapo Oslo, and (among other things) responsible for the deportation of 532 Norwegian Jews: 'In 1942, Auschwitz was a name unknown to him.'[20] Richard Hartmann, subordinate to Adolf Eichmann in the 'Central Office for Jewish Emigration' in the Reich Security Main Office and involved in the refusal of emigration requests of Jews from Germany, France, Croatia and the Netherlands, as well as in their deportation:

> At the time, the fate of the Jews deported to the East was unknown to him [...]. He [...] assumed that the Jews deported from Düsseldorf and Croatia too, were put up in camps and would emigrate en masse after the end of the war. He had not known at the time of the *Final Solution of the Jews* in the sense of physical annihilation.[21]

Much the same applied to Hartmann's colleague, Fritz Wöhrn, responsible for the incarceration of thousands of Jews in concentration camps and for refusing the release of foreign passports to Jews in The Netherlands. Despite having worked in the 'Jewish department' from 1940 until the end of the war, Wöhrn had allegedly 'hardly noticed anything' of the discriminatory measures taken against the Jews. Although before his judges he admitted having known of the 'evacuation of the Jews to the East', he never knew or suspected that this had implied their systematic extermination: 'He had only heard of this after the war, through the press.'[22]

And for the 'Jewish expert' in Berlin and Italy, Friedrich Bosshammer, things were no different:

> Until the end of the war he remained of the opinion that his work only involved the evacuation of the Jews to the East for the purpose of labour employment. [...] True enough, he did read the reports of the foreign press about the killing of Jews and he also noticed that the frequency and incisiveness of these reports increased more and more from the beginning of 1942 until the end of 1943. Thus, there was an account of October 1942 which stated that a million Jews had already been murdered in Europe in a ghastly manner. Even as they mentioned the mass gassings of Jews at the end of 1942, he did, however, not believe these reports and considered them as pure atrocity propaganda.[23]

In France, the deportations were organized by the deputy of Commander of the Security Police Helmut Knochen, Kurt Lischka, in cooperation with Herbert Hagen (personal assistant to Higher SS- and Police Leader Carl Oberg) and 'Jewish Expert', Ernst Heinrichsohn. During their trial before the Cologne court in 1979/1980, Lischka refused to say anything, but his position was undoubtedly similar to that of his co-defendants, Hagen and Heinrichsohn, who also had had no idea what they inflicted on the French Jews:

> [Hagen:] From the reports presented to him he saw that the Jews were deported. He has, however, not asked himself what would happen to them. He assumed that the Jews were taken to a camp for the purpose of a later transfer to a Jewish state [...]. Only after his departure from Paris [August 1944, DdM] has he heard about what had happened to the Jews in Auschwitz. If he had heard earlier what really happened to the Jews, he would have resigned.
>
> [Heinrichsohn:] He was convinced that the people who were squeezed into the [train] wagons, went to the East for labour employment. This was also the answer he received when he asked about the destination of the trains. Since he was still very young [22, DdM], he gave it no more thought. Only after the war has he heard what really happened to the Jews.[24]

Their colleague, Kurt Asche, who directed the deportation of the Belgian Jews from his headquarters at the 'Jewish department' in Brussels:

> During the entire proceedings the defendant has denied having known that the majority of the deported Jews were killed at Auschwitz. In this respect, he has stated that he merely knew that there were Buna and petrol factories in Auschwitz; with regard to the rest he had no knowledge of Auschwitz. It is indeed true that women and children and old people were also deported to Auschwitz. As far as this is concerned it is possible that Eichmann had said that 10 % of those unfit to work could be sent along. He has never asked himself what would happen to those unable to work. That was something he did not care about as he had after all nothing to do with what happened at Auschwitz. He also never gave it a thought where the many Jews went.[25]

And finally there was the retired ministerial councilor, count Von Korff. During the active part of his career, Korff had been head of the Security Police in Châlons-sur-Marne and had deported the local Jews to Drancy (and beyond):

> According to his conviction, the word *'Endlösung'* ['Final Solution'], was only understandable in its full meaning to insiders. For himself the word implied that the German occupied territories had to be made *judenfrei* ['cleared of Jews'] and that these people had to be transferred to the East for employment. According to his idea that also meant that the Jews were not to be repatriated after the war, but would be settled in some kind of territory, of which several were discussed. As far as the deportation of children or infants was concerned, he did not consider the separation of families useful.[26]

These examples of alleged unawareness on the part of those who appeared before a court of law constitute a mere fraction of the large reservoir of similar excuses employed by the deportation specialists and other mass murder accomplices of the Third Reich. Under the skilful conductorship of the legal counselor whom we have already met earlier on – former SS-Obergruppenführer Werner Best – all of them, sang the libretto of ignorance at the top of their voices.[27]

Much to their dismay, however, there were two among them who stepped out of line. These were the former Commander of the Security Police in the Netherlands, Dr. Wilhem Harster, and his subordinate, head of section IV B 4 (*Judenreferat*), Wilhelm Zoepf. In 1967 both men were tried in Munich for their role in the deportation of the Jews from the Netherlands.[28] To the surprise of many, Harster and Zoepf admitted to having known the fate of the deported Jews. And Harster also explained why, despite this knowledge, he had not chosen to cease his cooperation in the deportations. It was because he had left the responsibility for the 'gruesome events' with those 'who had ordered them'. Added to this was his deep-rooted conditioning to obedience as duty-bound policeman, which prevented even the mere thought of abandoning his position. And then there was also the circumstance that Germany was entangled in a struggle for life and death which caused so many casualties and destruction that one hardly cared any more for the fate of others. Finally, of course, there were also the effects of the anti-Jewish propaganda and the increasing desensitization towards concepts of justice and injustice. As far as his criminal responsibility was concerned, Harster commented as follows in his closing statement before the court:

> My guilt consists of the fact that, despite everything, I continued and remained at my post. What I have said about that is not meant as an excuse but as an explanation. Nothing of it was, however, suited to justify myself. Substitutive, I would like to ask the representatives of the accessory private prosecution (*Nebenklage*) to accept my profound feelings of remorse and sadness.

And to this, his co-defendant, Zoepf, added:

> I know that I have failed, measured by the only principles which, today, I consider just. If I search for the reasons of my failure, they cannot take away my guilt. Thus, there is nothing left for me than to admit my guilt over my part in the deportations and, again, to express my remorse and sadness over the victims.

Whether or not we are to take these admissions of guilt and sorrow seriously need not concern us here. Opinions on that will probably differ forever. What matters, however, are the reasons which withheld Harster and Zoepf to give up their positions once they realized what they were doing. These reasons were no different from those of Speer and were rooted in the very same concern for their positions. And, again, this concern was not given in by Harster's or Zoepf's fear for execution or concentration camp confinement, but by anxiety over their inevitable ostracism and demotion from the ranks of their peers. Like Speer and their fellow deportation experts, Harster and Zoepf stifled the voice of their conscience because it demanded a price which they were simply not willing to pay, namely the sacrifice of their immediate self-interest. On the third day of the trial, Willy Zoepf left no doubt about this in his statement before the court:

'I have often pored over these things. But I was too cowardly to procure final certainty over the events. For then, I would have had to take action. I was therefore glad to hide behind my administrative work. To be sure, I wanted to get away from the Judenreferat. *But it was the first civil service office appointment in my life and I wanted first to prove myself in it for a couple of years.*'[29]

3 'That which must not, cannot be' (I)

In the light of the unspeakable crimes in which they participated, the sober observations of the Hamburg judge on the common motives of his defendants, cited earlier, are certainly shocking. But whoever takes the trouble of casting a glance in the court rooms of the post-war mass murder trials, will find that they were indeed not populated by fuming 'idealists', perverted sadists or otherwise derailed representatives of the societal fringe, but by defendants whose character traits, ambitions, overall background history and psychology were not dissimilar to those of their environment. One could call them 'ordinary men', or perhaps more accurately, 'ordinary Germans'. But whatever the terminology, it is clear that they hardly matched the profile of those of whom one suspected the evil for which they were tried and of which – for the most part – they were guilty. This contradiction between the format of the criminals on the one hand, and that of their crimes on the other, has been emphasized here on a number of occasions. In fact, however, it turns out to be little more than a measly paradox. And our earlier observation that one searches in vain with these criminals for anything in their personal histories to indicate that they were somehow 'predestined' for their crimes, was certainly also premature. For as the words of the Hamburg judge illustrate, these indications were definitely present. That we tend to overlook them has everything to do with their all too common everyday appearance; an appearance which one could easily also call 'banal'.

This qualification carries a flip-side, however, which makes clear why it has always been met with such hesitancy and even categorical rejection. For if the perpetrators' behavior cannot be adequately explained by their special nature, we are, of course, compelled to look for the answers in the circumstances under which they committed their crimes. But if these circumstances were the main determinants of their criminal conduct, the obvious question springs to mind with which Christopher Browning concluded the case-study of his murderous policemen: 'If the men of Reserve

'That which must not, cannot be' (I) 99

Police Battalion 101 could become killers under such circumstances, what group of men cannot?'[30] And the implicit answer to this question appears unacceptable to those who consider themselves immune for such conditions.

In an impressively compelling fashion the West German prosecution efforts of Nazi criminals have demonstrated the dubiousness of this self-complacent assumption. During the heydays of these efforts, around the middle of the nineteen sixties, German criminologist and criminal law expert Herbert Jäger already emphasized their importance in his still unsurpassed study on crimes under totalitarian rule:

> Even though it did not belong to their primary task, one should realize in this respect the contribution made to the clarification of the past by precisely these trials and the criminological interpretation of the crimes. If we only had at our disposal the literature, the analyses of the humanities and political sciences, the biographies of prominent Nazis and the documentation, the era of National-Socialist rule would appear to us as one enormous and past natural disaster: names such as Auschwitz and Majdanek, Belzec and Treblinka would appear to us today as the designations of earthquakes or volcanic eruptions, symbols of a collective, transpersonal event, in which, indeed, many people had been entangled, but which could not be measured by individual categories. An awareness of the way in which many individuals, living among us today, participated in them, would thus hardly have emerged.[31]

Apart from a few (very) old specimens, the individuals Jäger referred to have in the meantime disappeared from our midst due to the inexorable laws of biology. But the documented heritage of their criminal prosecution and trials has been preserved in the archives. And this archival material indeed illustrates how important these post-war prosecution efforts are for our understanding of this particular criminal past and its actors. Without the Jerusalem trial, Adolf Eichmann would undoubtedly have remained just as much the mythical figure Josef Mengele is destined to stay in our imagination forever. The difference in our perception of both criminals is determined by the fact that the first one was tracked down, captured and duly brought to trial, whereas the latter managed to escape this fate. And it was his criminal prosecution which ultimately reduced the 'expediter of death' to human proportions, with the properties which make up the characteristics of his kind.

Even nearly sixty years after the Jerusalem trial, however, many still appear to have difficulty with these characteristics and prefer to model

Eichmann and his associates after the Laoconian image. In a way, this persistent preference for the patho-ideological profile reminds us of the experiences of Arthur Koestler and his 'screamers'. For just as public opinion could not bring itself to accept the reality of Hitler's genocide at the time, so, decades later, it still has considerable trouble to face the true nature of its practitioners.

This becomes particularly clear from the occasional flare-up of the controversy surrounding Hannah Arendt's famous banality thesis. Among the latest contributions to this controversy is the one from the German philosopher Bettina Stangneth. In her book on Eichmann Stangneth aims for a drastic correction of Arendt's thesis.[32] Essentially, she does so by pointing out that Eichmann remained a ferocious anti-Semite throughout his life and, as a sort of grand manipulator of the truth, managed to mislead many (and especially Arendt and her likes) about his real personality in the Jerusalem court room. To many of Arendt's contemporary critics this has turned Stangneth into something of a celebrated authority in the field. But whoever takes the trouble of seriously considering her arguments cannot help but wonder where this general enthusiasm over her findings comes from. For Stangneth's discovery of Eichmann's post-war comments are certainly illustrative of his Jew-hatred and murderous zeal. But none of them actually comes close to the most extreme statement in this respect with which we had already been familiar for decades. This, of course, is the statement – cited earlier here – which his subordinate, Dieter Wisliceny, presented to the judges at Nuremberg: 'He said he would leap laughing into the grave because the feeling that he had 5 million people on his conscience would be for him a source of extraordinary satisfaction.' This 'confession' of Eichmann's murderous fanaticism was not only already common knowledge at the time of his trial, but was also – remarkably enough – not even disputed by the defendant himself.[33] As far as this aspect of Eichmann is concerned then, Stangneth's revelations contain no news and certainly do not invalidate any of Arendt's conclusions about him.

What about his 'acting performance' in Jerusalem then? That Eichmann was a compulsory fantasist escaped no one who witnessed him in court or read his interrogation accounts, least of all Hannah Arendt. Whoever doubts that should (re-)read her book with the attention it deserves. But those who, for whatever reason, nonetheless refuse to be convinced by her observations, might perhaps be persuaded by the Israeli police officer who spent months with Eichmann in the interrogation room and at no point fell for the melodramatic talents of his interlocutor. With accurate precision Avner Less pinpointed Eichmann as the blustering opportunist, 'obsessed with the idea to make a career, regardless how and to what price.'[34]

In fact, and as the findings of his judges underline, Eichmann's attempts to present himself as the guiltless actor of a criminal drama beyond his control fooled no one. And this brings us back to the reason for the popularity of Stangneth's message. Surprisingly enough – and perhaps unintended, but with striking precision none the less – the author herself provides us with the answer. She does so when she addresses the puzzling phenomenon that many surviving victims recalled encounters with Eichmann that had never taken place in reality. Stangneth explains this remarkable fact as follows:

> It obviously belongs to the human mechanisms for self-preservation, that we simply cannot or will not imagine a person playing a significant role in decisions about our fate, as a paltry figure. Whoever experiences sorrow, humiliation and loss does not also wants to be the victim of pure mediocrity, because the idea that a zero holds power over us is even more unbearable than that someone holds power over us. This mechanism in turn distorts a clear view of the perpetrator.[35]

What Stangneth exposes here is precisely the mental 'mechanism' which frustrates the acceptance of Arendt's notion of the banality of evil: the inability to accept 'pure mediocrity' as the personification of evil. It is a prime example of a phenomenon social psychologists have dubbed 'cognitive dissonance'. It occurs in situations in which reality collides head on with cherished personal beliefs, values and desires. The tension which results from such a collision is usually solved by the denial of reality. We will return to this subject later, but we came across it earlier on in Chaim Kaplan's comment on the desperate attempts of his fellow ghetto inhabitants to deny their approaching doom, as well as in the Koestler example. As unacceptable as it was for many contemporaries to face genocidal reality, so it is apparently impossible for Stangneth and her supporters to match mediocrity with mass extermination.

Within contemporary circles of Stangneth-inspired 'Arendt-bashers' this inability expresses itself in the misrepresentation of Arendt's findings, in order to disqualify them through the introduction of a variety of pseudo-sagacious counterarguments. From those who (at best) have only browsed through Arendt's book on Eichmann, one should perhaps expect little different. But if even internationally renowned scholars adopt such an approach, it seems worth noticing. Thus, in his relatively recent study, '*The killing compartments. The mentality of mass murder*', Dutch sociologist Abram de Swaan, for example, has this to say on the subject:

> Were the perpetrators banal? Arendt's thesis on the 'banality of evil' does not stand critical scrutiny, certainly not as applied to Adolf Eichmann or other Nazi leaders, nor for that matter to the rank-and-file killers.[36]

In the Dutch version of the book, De Swaan is even slightly more precise as he refers in this connection to 'the facts' that contradict Arendt's thesis.[37] This, of course, prompts the question after the 'critical scrutiny' of 'the facts' which allegedly disprove Arendt's position. Unfortunately, however, one does not find the answer in De Swaan's book. And this is no surprise. For as his references show, De Swaan has not taken the trouble of personally investigating these facts on the basis of the sole source we have at our disposal in this connection: the judicial documentation of the prosecution and trials of the perpetrators. Had he done so, he would have discovered that the 'critical scrutinizers' who are familiar with the facts better than anyone else, have underlined Arendt's views time and again. One more example from a Hamburg judge pondering over the criminal nature of his defendants:

> Whoever looks at the Nazi-crimes – massacres of human beings without comprehensible motive, without a trace of reasonable cause – is forced to the conclusion that no punishment can be hard enough for them. If one takes a look at the perpetrators, however, this surely changes nothing about the judgement on the crimes, but the assumption that behind these unimaginable crimes stand corresponding actors – cruel, sadistic and driven by an extraordinary criminal energy – is generally not confirmed. Criminal types such as the SSPF Lublin, Globocnik, or similar sadists in subordinate functions, who have become known through Nazi trials, are not representative, they are exceptions. It is, on the contrary, the Banality of Evil which is so shocking.[38]

Apparently, however, De Swaan does not recognize the critical expertise of the judges and distrusts their sources of information, i.e. the records of the criminal investigations. For according to De Swaan, these prosecution records have a clear tendency to distort the facts and present a false image of reality:

> Judicial evidence tends to reinforce the impression of depersonalization in the perpetrators. Before their judges, the men minimized their initiatives, convictions,

'That which must not, cannot be' (I)   103

emotions, ambitions, and desires. Their personalities pale in the process. They come to look more and more like Hannah Arendt's version of Eichmann, and for the same reasons he chose to present himself in that manner. What is often lost in the trial documentation is the individual diversity in dealing with the genocidal situation.[39]

Again, it remains somewhat of a mystery how De Swaan reaches such firm conclusions, as he has, obviously, never set eyes on the records on which they are based. But let us, for argument's sake, assume that he somehow learned of them. How then should we interpret his observations?

As far as the 'paled personalities' of the defendants are concerned, one is advised to read the detailed characterizations of them in their trial judgments. They are far too extensive to be cited here, but they leave no doubt about the fact that their judges were the last to fall for such 'mystification'.[40] And then there is, of course, De Swaan's observation that the trial documentation lacks 'the individual diversity in dealing with the genocidal situation'. The factual inaccuracy of this observation is underlined immediately by the author himself, as he describes the variety of perpetrator conduct within the genocidal universe:

> Some men were 'willing executioners', volunteering for the Jew hunt, eager to join the roundups and the shootings and given to haphazard cruelty (and sometimes equally random kindness, too, since unpredictable favours on a whim would even better display their supreme power over other human beings). Other men limited their participation to the tasks that were explicitly demanded from them, without much enthusiasm, but without objection either. And, finally, there were men who tried to exploit what little room for maneuver they perceived in order to stay away from the roundups, forced marches, and executions.[41]

This characterization of the various types of perpetrator behavior stems directly from the sources which De Swaan distrusts. And, again, this is no surprise, since these sources are in fact the only ones which contain substantial information on the varieties of such behavior. Nor is it all that surprising that De Swaan disregards the other 'facts' contained in this judicial documentation. For they would force him in a direction which the Hamburg judge so clearly expressed and which De Swaan obviously finds unacceptable. It does show, however, that his difficulty with Arendt's banality thesis is not so much inspired by factual considerations as by other ones. And since he seems to share them with many of Arendt's opponents, there is good reason to take a closer look at them.

4 'That which must not, cannot be' (II)

From the moment when her book was first published, in May 1963, a number of crucial 'misunderstandings' determined the discourse on Hannah Arendt's vision of Adolf Eichmann. For the most part they have been cherished by her critics and, with remarkable tenacity, introduced time and again in any debate on the subject. By now, they have become firmly established ingredients of the controversy over Arendt's image of Eichmann; a controversy which continues to pop up now and then, here and there, even after more than half a century since the appearance of Arendt's book. For anyone familiar with this ongoing controversy, it is obvious then that she struck an open nerve.

Originally, this was not so much caused by her presentation of the defendant as by her provocative criticism of the Jewish and Zionist leaders and organizations, which were supposed to have facilitated Eichmann's crimes. In her polemics with Walter Laqueur, in January 1966, Arendt complained that even before her book came out, the Anti-Defamation League had already warned its organizations in the US about the possible damage of her views in this respect for the Jewish reputation.[42] In addition, the ADL had recommended its own list of criticisms to book reviewers for consideration in their comments. The list consisted of five main points, none of which – according to Arendt – presented her arguments in a fair and correct manner. Whether this constituted a deliberate attempt to discredit the author and her book – Arendt herself referred to it as a 'war' – is of no further interest to us here. What is remarkable, however, is that the criticisms drawn up by the ADL have continued to dominate the debate on Arendt's book until this very day. And this particularly also applies to the subject of our interest here: Arendt's image of Adolf Eichmann.

So what does this image consist of? First, let us turn to the version that has been attributed to Arendt with persistent determination, but does not originate with her. This is the image listed as number one on the ADL's inventory: 'That Eichmann was, as he himself claimed, only a small cog in the extermination machinery.'[43] With De Swaan, for example, this becomes the image 'of an average bureaucrat, of just another number in the huge equation of the Nazi state.'[44] The person who appears here is indeed the indistinctive civil servant and soulless bureaucrat, who, devoid of any personal engagement thoughtlessly carries out the tasks given to him quite simply because his bureaucratic duty roster tells him to do so. This sterile, almost mechanical image of Eichmann as a randomly exchangeable component within Hitler's vast extermination machinery, was, however, not the invention of Hannah Arendt, nor indeed even of Eichmann himself (who considered it too unappreciative of his personal efforts). It was the invention of Eichmann's counsel, Dr. Robert Servatius.[45] To be fair, as defense attorney Servatius had little choice in the matter. For the favorite scenario of all Nazi criminals before their judges – *'nicht dabei und nichts gewusst'* ('wasn't there and knew nothing') – was clearly no option here, if only because his client never denied his involvement or his knowledge. This left Servatius with no alternative but to minimize Eichmann's contribution to the slaughter and picture him as a reluctant pawn in a drama steered by higher powers. From the outset, it was an effort which was destined to fail, just as the diametrically opposed one by prosecutor Gideon Hausner, who presented Eichmann as the omnipotent orchestrator of the Holocaust. For obvious reasons, neither of these simplifications found its way to the Jerusalem court's judgment.[46]

In Arendt's version of Eichmann, he is certainly also a bureaucratic executor of superior orders (which, after all, he in fact was). But at the same time she makes it very clear that he was definitely no insignificant or indifferent one.[47] Thus, in her chapter on the 'Duties of a Law-Abiding Citizen', Arendt identifies Eichmann's motives as she addresses his claim of having always lived in accordance with Kant's moral precepts, in particular with his definition of duty:

> it is true that Eichmann's unconscious distortion [of Kant's categorical imperative, DdM] agrees with what he himself called the version of Kant 'for the household use of the little man.' In this household use, all that is left of Kant's spirit is the demand that a man do more than obey the law, that he go beyond the mere call of obedience and identify his own will with the principle behind the law – the source from which the law sprang. In Kant's philosophy, that source was practical reason; in Eichmann's household use of him, it was the will of the Führer.[48]

This unconditional and determined adherence to the will of the Führer made Eichmann, in Arendt's view, into a dedicated and uncompromising murderer, who could only react with exasperated disbelief to Himmler's opportunistic cessation of the killing operation during the final months of the war. According to Eichmann's concept of duty, this was nothing short of a betrayal of the Führer's most sacrosanct principle. And indeed, as Arendt notes, such treason 'must have been a shattering experience for Eichmann.'[49]

Obviously, this interpretation of Eichmann's motives by Hannah Arendt is a far cry from Servatius' small-cog theory. And the huge gap that separates the two prompts the question why so many have nevertheless continued to identify Arendt's version with that of Eichmann's counsel. The answer to this question lies hidden behind the characteristics which Arendt attributed to Eichmann's personality. These characteristics did not apply to his deeds, but to his words. Thus, from beginning to end, Arendt's thesis of the banality of evil was exclusively based on Eichmann's verbal outpourings in the interrogation and court rooms. And, as anyone familiar with the thousands of pages which fill up the transcripts of his comments can confirm, this was indeed quite something. Compared to Adolf Eichmann, Franz Stangl was not only an extraordinarily frugal commentator but an example of precision and modesty. For with his melodramatic outbursts and self-justifications, denials of responsibility and bizarre *mea culpa*'s ('I carry great guilt, I know.... But I had nothing to do with the killing of the Jews.'[50]), Eichmann drove his interlocutors to despair on many occasions. This applied not least to the police officer we introduced earlier on, Avner Less. Less, who was born in Berlin and whose father had been deported to Auschwitz with one of the final transports, was compelled to listen to Eichmann's sentimental eulogy on the 'Franz-Josephinian' architectural beauty of the Lemberg train station, which struck his eye on the way back from witnessing a mass execution.[51] And who – 'with a courteous bow' – was presented Eichmann's personal notes ('Herr Hauptmann, may I offer you my memoirs?'), of which the nonsensical closing lines read as follows:

> Nothing is therefore left for me, but to repeat the same in front of the Court, accept the designated punishment and tell the coming generations that they are constantly to consider the final, horrible conclusion, which the Middle Ages that expired on 8 May 1945 was still in a position to present, as a warning guideline for their lives, so that they will finally be given peace on earth and harmony among all peoples of this earth. And I call out to the surviving and future youth, even though I realize full well that for the expulsion and killing of millions of Germans no one has yet been punished and certainly no one ever will.[52]

Understandably, Less dismissed these words as 'empty and insincere prattle' and asked himself in amazement, 'is this man completely dehumanized, does he then not recognize the perversity of this situation?'

Even according to her most celebrated contemporary critic, Bettina Stangneth, there are only few who studied Eichmann's interrogation and trial statements as meticulously as Hannah Arendt did.[53] And this analysis brought her to the conclusion that, with all his unconditional loyalty to his Führer's assignment, Eichmann was essentially no more than a buffoon; neither unintelligent nor untalented in ways, but a windbag, nonetheless. This was a shocking discovery indeed, but one which inescapably resulted from her acquaintance with the meaningless bombast which Eichmann kept repeating during his interrogation sessions and his trial. There are many highly illustrative examples of this in Arendt's book (up to and including Eichmann's final words beneath the gallows), and many more can be found in the interrogation records from which she took these examples. It remains therefore somewhat of a puzzle to understand how anyone familiar with them can seriously doubt the accuracy of Arendt's observations in this respect.

This particularly also applies to the 'thoughtlessness' with which, according to Arendt, Eichmann carried out his crimes. It was an opinion which, again, she shared with Avner Less. After his extended talks with him, Less concluded 'that Eichmann had obviously no understanding of the monstrosity of his crimes and that he did not feel even the remotest sign of remorse.'[54] Of course neither Arendt nor Less meant by this that Eichmann had had no idea that he shipped his victims to their deaths. Instead, both referred to his fundamental lack of appreciation of the exceptional nature of this crime. To some extent, their observation reminds us of that of Jesus' alleged uttering at the cross: 'Father forgive them, for they do not know what they are doing.' Clearly, in Eichmann's case Arendt and Less shared no sympathy for the opening words of this statement (see in this respect, Arendt's passionate plea for the imposition of the death penalty on Eichmann), but what followed certainly also applied to this Jerusalem defendant. For just as the murderers of Jesus had evidently not grasped the true meaning of their crime against the divine order, so Eichmann obviously failed to understand his profound abuse of its worldly counterpart, the bond of humanity.

Which brings us back to the objections against Arendt's view on Eichmann. Why does this view continue to provoke so much irritation and rejection? The answer comes from a man whose life's motto is of a disarming simplicity: 'that which must not, cannot be.'

5 Facing 'impossible' facts

Somewhat over a century ago, German author Christian Morgenstern wrote a short poem entitled *'Die unmögliche Tatsache'* or 'The Impossible Fact'.[55] It deals with an old man by the name of Palmström, who gets run over by a truck while crossing an intersection. Lying in the street, having barely survived the accident, Palmström ponders over the reasons why it had taken place. Finally, he comes up with the conclusion that it hasn't, because it shouldn't have: '*Weil nicht sein kann, was nicht sein darf*' ('since that which must not, cannot be'). Thus, by denying a reality that hit him full front, Palmström is the very champion of someone tackling a problem we referred to earlier as that of 'cognitive dissonance'.[56]

In this respect, Palmström could easily also be regarded as the very 'personification' of the opposition against Arendt's banality thesis. And he is certainly a formidable opponent, which is precisely what Hannah Arendt overlooked when she presented her image of Eichmann. For what she disregarded was the fact that Palmström and his like are not at all interested in a factual reading of the man in the Jerusalem dock. Instead, they prefer a version of the defendant which allows them to distance themselves as much as they possibly can from any resemblance with him. For heaven forbid, of course, that such likeness should exist. In a provocative way, Arendt's version of Eichmann collides head-on with such concerns. And this prompts countermeasures, even up to and including the defamation of its author and her arguments. Thus, accusations are hurled at Arendt which not only lack substance, but, moreover, show a marked personal animosity towards the author.

Whoever, like Arendt, calls attention to the banality of evil as personified by Eichmann, marks, of course, a personality characteristic, a psychological feature of the defendant. Or, as she herself put it: 'When I speak of the banality of evil, I do so only on the strictly factual level, pointing to a phenomenon which stared one in the face at the trial.'[57] Obviously, this aims at something entirely different from any trivialization of the evil for which Eichmann carried responsibility. But it is precisely this trivialization of which Arendt has been accused over and over again.[58] Such manipulation of her arguments leaves little doubt indeed about the hostility towards Arendt by her Palmström-inspired opponents.

The grounds for this hostility are to be found in the disconcerting consequences of Arendt's thesis. For even though she sought to limit her image of Adolf Eichmann to the defendant himself, she realized full well that it had implications which went far beyond the criminal in the Jerusalem dock: 'The trouble with Eichmann was precisely that so many were like him, and that the many were neither perverted nor sadistic, that they were, and still are, terribly and terrifyingly normal.'[59] And, again, her observation was shared wholeheartedly by Avner Less:

> The dreadful thing with all this, is that this Eichmann is no exception. There are many like him. [...] As harsh as it may sound and no matter how many will protest against it, but many among us are capable of playing a role like Eichmann. And so, Eichmann will turn into a symbol of evil.[60]

Outside Jerusalem, this symbol of evil materialized itself nowhere with such a perplexing recurrence and precision as in the post-war German court rooms. Here, the incarnate banality almost literally bulged out of the suspect benches in the shape of Eichmann's collaborators.[61] And this massive confirmation of the conclusions of Arendt and Less indeed forms a serious challenge to the self-complacency of Palmström and his allies. For after all, if the banality thesis turns out to be accurate and if its relevance reaches far beyond the person of Adolf Eichmann alone, it is food for some disturbing thoughts.

Those who wish to quell these thoughts regularly present their ultimate objection against Arendt's thesis in its crudest form: if she is right, everyone is 'Eichmann' and thus by nature inclined to his crimes. It is a counter-argument with guaranteed effect, as the critics know their audience well and are keenly aware of the general repugnance with which this idea will be met. Thus we read with De Swaan:

> I very much doubt that I, or most of my readers for that matter, on being brought into the killing site would have started, like automatons, clubbing, knifing, shooting, gassing people to death by the thousands, for weeks and months at a stretch.[62]

Of course, De Swaan knows very well that no sane person (least of all Hannah Arendt[63]) ever suggested anything like it, but the very fact that he presents his readers with this 'consolation' nonetheless, shows his marked susceptibility to Palmström's logic.

Wholly aside from all overstrained reactions, however, it is clear that the conclusion that Adolf Eichmann and his likes distinguished themselves above all by their conventional and even banal personalities, has serious consequences for our self-image. The stretched out post-war prosecution of Nazi criminals shows that this banality had a great many faces and without doubt Eichmann's was the most sensationally melodramatic among them. But their stories all share one thing: the commonplaceness of their self-centered psychology. It is this instinct for plain egoism that has been emphasized here over and over again, as it forms the ultimate key to the question of Michael Marrus as to 'why so many followed Hitler down his murderous path.' Within an environment exclusively controlled by Nazism, this blank opportunism became, as we argued, the ideal ally of a criminal regime and the chief engine of murderous conduct by state orders. And the recurring emergence and central importance of this factor in the perpetrators' profiles confront us with an unpleasant message indeed. For if such a commonly shared human attribute formed the catalyst of genocidal behavior, the face of evil takes on a nasty familiarity, of course. Refusing to acknowledge this familiarity ignores one of the most crucial lessons of Hitler's genocidal enterprise: the one about ourselves.

Postscript: the measure of all things

> We do not know ourselves, we knowledgeable people, we are ignorant about ourselves. And there is good reason for that. For we have never tried to find out who we are. How then could it ever happen that, one day, we would discover ourselves?
>
> Friedrich Nietzsche, *On the genealogy of morality*

In the Wertheim Park in Amsterdam one finds an impressive Auschwitz monument by Dutch sculptor and writer Jan Wolkers, lying flat on the ground. With his horizontal construction of broken mirrors Wolkers sought to express that, after the horrors which had taken place on the earth beneath it, there could no longer be a whole reflection of heaven. Next to the monument there is an upright glass slab with the words 'Nooit meer Auschwitz' ['Auschwitz, never again'].

The message implies, of course, that Auschwitz and the genocidal slaughter it represents were no unique phenomena. For it recognizes the possibility of repetition. The pressing question then would be how to avoid such a recurrence? Surely, by far the best answer would consist of the banishment of all forms of racial hatred, anti-Semitism and xenophobia. And this is undoubtedly a commendable mission. But the disturbing fact is that we have made depressingly little progress in this field over the past seven post-war decades. This failure is remarkable in itself, as 'Auschwitz' was generally considered as the ultimate expression of man's potential for inhumanity. Thus, we should perhaps consider the lack of progress in this respect a disturbing comment on yet another of man's powerful potentials: the inclination to ignore his darkest side.

That the argument of 'Auschwitz' failed to sufficiently impress the post-war generations to which it was addressed, remains, however, a fact to be faced. Thus, given that there is apparently no ideal solution to the problem, is there then perhaps something like an alternative, a 'second-best' answer to the question? There is indeed and it is called the '*Rechtsstaat*', the state governed by law and justice. It is the socio-political construct of legally defined checks and balances which aims to protect its citizens against governmental abuse of power. Without doubt, it is the single most impressive invention of mankind in its quest for collective self-control. Ever since the Age of Enlightenment, key principles of this *Rechtsstaat* have been introduced into the state fabric of most Western countries and, especially after World War II, many of them also found their way into a variety of international organizations. As a man-made defense structure against authoritarian arbitrariness, the *Rechtsstaat* is, however, no magic formula and certainly also no unconditional safeguard against a recurrence of something such as 'Auschwitz'. For it is neither infallible nor self-evident. It remains under constant threat from its many powerful opponents and its defense and maintenance are reliant on the support of those it aims to protect.

To mobilize this support the *Rechtsstaat* needs compelling arguments. Among the most significant of these is obviously the one from recent history; more in particular from the history of the one *Rechtsstaat*, the ruin of which we know so much about: the German republic of the interbellum period. Historians have studied its many flaws and described the incremental stages which led to its demolition. And even today their accounts continue to form spine-chilling reading, particularly when one realizes the devastating effects these developments had on so many ordinary civilians. For it is one thing to read about the political machinations of the power-hungry elites and the legal acts and decrees which ended classical political and civil liberties in Germany and endowed its police state with unlimited powers, but it is quite another to learn about the immense sufferings which they brought upon their helpless victims. Thus, only the stories of these flesh-and-blood victims allow us to even begin to imagine what Hitler's *Unrechtsstaat* really stood for. And, as Arthur Koestler rightly pointed out, when trying to grasp the true meaning of the process, it is very much 'the detail which counts.'

This equally holds true for the other end of the spectrum. In order to understand the *modus operandi* of Hitler's criminal state, it is important to familiarize us with its collaborators. And this is why their post-war prosecution and trials should matter to us. For it is only through the efforts to bring them to justice that we are in a position to get to know them in a more or less intimate fashion. Over the past three quarters of a century, these efforts have resulted in much information on their backgrounds, their personalities, their 'route to crime' and their behavior in the service of their Führer's criminal state. By far the most detailed information on all of these aspects stems from the West German prosecution efforts. Whatever their flaws – and they are considerable –, the extended attempts of the West German judiciary to bring the Nazi criminals to justice have taught us some highly important lessons about them. Above all, they have shown us in a most impressive way that the horrors committed during the twelve years of Hitler's Third Reich were entirely man-made and that the socio-psychological profiles of those responsible resemble ours to a far greater extent than we would like. It is therefore hardly surprising that the unease about such a resemblance remains widespread. Its recognition, however, is a precondition for any serious attempt to avoid a recurrence of the horrors for which Wolkers' monument of broken mirrors seeks to warn us.

Which finally brings us back to its positioning. Had he put his memorial of disfigured reflections upright, it would have impressed upon its passers-by that this marred reflection applied to them as well. And with it, Wolkers would have directed his *mene tekel* at the only address that really matters. For the citation with which Alan Bullock closed off his early biography of Adolf Hitler seems particularly well in place here, as well: '*si monumentum requiris, circumspice*' – 'if you seek a monument, look around you.'[1]

Appendix

List of German trial cases used in this study (by JuNSV number)

Editorial note: In accordance with German privacy laws, the names of the defendants in the JuNSV series had to be abbreviated in all instances in which defendants had not been sentenced to death or to life imprisonment, or to a so-called *Zuchthausstrafe* (penitentiary). I have adhered to this rule in the list below, unless the full names of the defendants have, in the mean time, been disclosed in newspapers and other publications on the subject and are thus commonly known, and only in so far as they are relevant within the context of this book. In all other instances the abbreviated names such as given in the JuNSV series have been maintained. For more information on the JuNSV project, see www.expostfacto.nl

Case number: 017
Volume: I
Pages: 303–379
Court decision(s):
District Court Frankfurt/M. 21 March 1947
District Court of Appeal Frankfurt/M. 20 October 1948
Defendants:
Borkowski, Margarethe Hermine *2½ Years*
Ge. born St., Lina *Acquittal*
G., Hubert *Acquittal*
Gorgass, Hans Bodo *Death Sentence*
Hä., Elfriede *Acquittal*
Härtle, Benedikt *3½ Years*
H., Paul *Acquittal*
Huber, Irmgard *8 Years*
L., Maximilian Friedrich *Acquittal*
Lückoff, Wilhelm *3 Years 1 Month*
Moos, Erich Karl Friedrich *4 Years*
Reuter, Paul *4½ Years*

R., Hildegard *Acquittal*
D., Fritz *Acquittal*
Schm., Margot *Acquittal*
Schrankel, Agnes *3½ Years*
Sc. born M., Johanna *Acquittal*
Se. born Wa., Ingeborg *Acquittal*
S., Paula *Acquittal*
T. born S., Judith *Acquittal*
Thomas, Lydia *5 Years*
U., Elisabeth *Acquittal*
Wahlmann, Adolf *Death Sentence*
W. geb. Wo., Elisabeth *Acquittal*
Zielke, Christel *3 Years 9 Months*
Country where the crime was committed: Germany
Crime Location: Mental Institution Hadamar
Agency: Medical, nursing, administrative and technical staff mental institution Hadamar (*Euthanasie-Aktion*)
Subject of the proceedings: Killing of mentally disabled patients by means of toxic gas and poisonous injections

Case number: 212
Volume: VI
Pages: 543–560
Court decision(s):
District Court Berlin, 8 May 1950
Chamber Court, 11 November 1950
Defendants:
Bauer, Erich Hermann *Death Sentence*
Country where the crime was committed: Poland
Crime Location: Sobibor
Agency: Detainment Center Staff Sobibor
Subject of the proceedings: Mass killing of Jews by the defendant, who was nicknamed '*Gasmeister*' of Sobibor, as well as mishandling and shooting of individual Jewish prisoners

Case number: 500
Volume: XVII

Pages: 1–50
Court decision(s):
District Court Düsseldorf, 3 September 1965
Federal High Court of Justice, 30 June 1970
Defendants:
Kremer, Johann Paul *10 Years*
Country where the crime was committed: Poland
Crime Location: Auschwitz concentration camp
Agency: Detainment Center Staff Auschwitz concentration camp
Subject of the proceedings: Criminal offences performed by a camp physician in Auschwitz. Participation in altogether 15 'special actions' (*Sonderaktionen*), during which Jewish prisoners arriving in Auschwitz were killed in the gas chambers by means of Zyklon B. Participation in a number of executions of Polish civilians at the execution site (*Genickschussanlage*). Killing of 6 female prisoners who were supposed to have taken part in a revolt in the Budy penal camp for women, by means of phenol-injections into the heart. Selection of ill prisoners during 'medical roll-calls' (*Arztvorstellungen*) in the out-patient department (*Ambulanzraum*); the selected patients were killed by phenol-injections. Selection of ill prisoners in the 'patients' quarters' for gassing.

Case number: 580
Volume: XX
Pages: 379–504
Court decision(s):
District Court München II, 30 September 1964
Federal High Court of Justice, 26 October 1965
Defendants:
Wolff, Karl Friedrich Otto *15 Years*
Country where the crime was committed: Ukraine
Crime Location: Winniza
Agency: *Reichsführer*-SS Personal staff
Subject of the proceedings: Complicity in the mass killing of the Warsaw Jews by intervening with the Under-Secretary of State of the Reich Ministry for Transport, in order to secure the availability of deportation trains to the extermination camp of Treblinka.

Case number: 596
Volume: XXII
Pages: 1–238
Court decision(s):
District Court Münster, 29 November 1960
Defendants:
Franz, Kurt Hubert *Life Sentence*
Horn, Richard Otto *Acquittal*
Lambert, Erwin Hermann *4 Years*
Matthes, Heinrich Arthur *Life Sentence*
Mentz, Willi *Life Sentence*
Miete, August Wilhelm *Life Sentence*
Münzberger, Gustav *12 Years*
Rum, Franz Albert Otto *3 Years (died before the judgment became final)*
Stadie, Otto *7 Years*
Suchomel, Franz *6 Years*
Country where the crime was committed: Poland
Crime Location: Treblinka
Agency: Detainment Center Staff Treblinka
Subject of the proceedings: Gassing of at least 700,000 Jewish men, women and children as well as of Sinti and Roma. Fatal mishandling, shooting, slaying and hanging of individual prisoners as well as mangling and killing of prisoners by 'Barry' the deputy camp commander's dog.

Case number: 641
Volume: XXV
Pages: 15–51
Court decision(s):
District Court Hagen, 20 December 1966
Defendants:
Fuchs, Erich Fritz *4 Years*
Country where the crime was committed: Poland
Crime Location: Sobibor
Agency: Detainment Center Staff Sobibor
Subject of the proceedings: Installing and tuning of an engine, whose exhaust fumes were led into the gas chamber. 'Trial gassing' of about

30 Jewish women as well as subsequent gassing of Jews arriving in 3–4 transports. Instruction of camp supervisor Bauer – cf. Case Number 212 – on how to operate the engine.

Case number: 642
Volume: XXV
Pages: 53–252
Court decision(s):
District Court Hagen, 20 December 1966
Federal High Court of Justice, 25 March 1971
Defendants:
Dubois, Karl Werner *3 Years*
Frenzel, Karl August Wilhelm *Life sentence*
Ittner, Alfred *4 Years*
Jührs, Robert Emil Franz Xaver *Acquittal*
Lachmann, Erich Gustav Willi *Acquittal*
Lambert, Erwin Hermann *3 Years*
Schütt, Hans-Heinz Friedrich Karl *Acquittal*
Unverhau, Heinrich *Acquittal*
Wolf, Franz *8 Years*
Zierke, Ernst *Acquittal*
Country where the crime was committed: Poland
Crime Location: Sobibor
Agency: Detainment Center Staff Sobibor
Subject of the proceedings: Mass gassing and single killings of altogether at least 150,000 Jewish civilians as well as of Red Army soldiers.

Case number: 645
Volume: XXV
Pages: 393–651
Court decision(s):
District Court München II, 24 February 1967
Defendants:
Harster, Dr. Wilhelm *15 Years*
Slo., Gertrud *5 Years*
Zoepf, Wilhelm *9 Years*
Country where the crime was committed: The Netherlands

Crime Location: The Hague
Agency: Security Police in The Netherlands
Subject of the proceedings: Organization of the disenfranchisement and of the arrest and deportation to Auschwitz and Sobibor of the Jewish population in the Netherlands.

Case number: 659
Volume: XXVI
Pages: 585–832
Court decision(s):
District Court Cologne, 30 October 1967
Federal High Court of Justice, 27 October 1969
Defendants:
Schul., Karl *15 Years*
Streitwieser, Anton *Life sentence + 7 Years*
Country where the crime was committed: Austria
Crime Location: Concentration camps Mauthausen, Gusen, Wien-Floridsdorf, Wien-Mödling (Hinterbrühl), along the road of the evacuation march from Wien-Mödling to Mauthausen
Agency: Detainment Center Staff concentration camp Mauthausen
Subject of the proceedings: Killing of thousands of prisoners by shooting, mishandling, gassing and by way of lethal injections as well as through selections within the context of *Aktion 14f13*. Killing of 47 Allied paratroopers in the camp's quarry.

Case number: 692
Volume: XXX
Pages: 413–705
Court decision(s):
District Court Hagen, 29 October 1968
Federal High Court of Justice 6 August 1970
Defendants:
Gro., Alfons *6 Years*
Jentzsch, Bruno Wolfgang Heinz *Life sentence*
Klu., Helmut Arthur Hermann *8 Years*
Sti., Wilhelm *Acquittal*
Country where the crime was committed: Austria

Crime Location: Concentration camp Gusen I
Agency: Detainment Center Staff concentration camp Gusen I
Subject of the proceedings: Killing of crippled and ill prisoners by means of so-called drowning-actions (*Totbadeaktionen*).

Case number: 670
Volume: XXVII
Pages: 525–650
Court decision(s):
District Court Hamburg, 8 April 1968
Federal High Court of Justice, 7 April 1970
Defendants:
Boc., Friedrich Rudolf Heinrich *no punishment imposed*
Brä., Alfred Max Emil *no punishment imposed*
Doo., Bruno John Christian *no punishment imposed*
Dos., Max Emil *no punishment imposed*
Gat., Erwin August Willy *no punishment imposed*
Gie., Wilhelm *no punishment imposed*
Woh., Julius Franz *8 Years*
Country where the crime was committed: Poland
Crime Location: Jozefow, Konskowola, Serokomla, Miedzyrzec, Lomazy, Komarowka, Parczew
Agency: Police Battalion 101 (Police Regiment 25)
Subject of the proceedings: Single and mass shootings, ghetto clearances and deportations within the context of the so-called *Aktion Reinhard*, in the Lublin district.

Case number: 673
Volume: XXVIII
Pages: 17–165
Court decision(s):
District Court Bamberg, 2 May 1968
District Court Nürnberg-Fürth, 17 March 1952
Federal High Court of Justice, 16 April 1953
Federal High Court of Justice, 27 October 1971
Defendants:
Rademacher, Franz *3½ Years*

Country where the crime was committed: Germany, Serbia
Crime Location: Berlin, Belgrade
Agency: Ministry of Foreign Affairs
Subject of the proceedings: Pressuring German institutions and governments allied with Germany, to shoot Jews imprisoned in Serbia and to deport Jews from Belgium, Germany, France, Croatia, the Netherlands and Rumania to concentration camps in Poland and to prevent their emigration to Palestine.

Case number: 678
Volume: XXIX
Pages: 311–408
Court decision(s):
District Court Bochum, 5 June 1968
Defendants:
Hac., Anton *Acquittal*
Kir., Erich *Acquittal*
Kra., Hermann *Acquittal*
La., Johann *Acquittal*
Pet., Otto *Acquittal*
Ple., Wilhelm *Acquittal*
Sac., Robert *Acquittal*
Sie., Erwin *Acquittal*
Wa., Dr. Oskar Karl Eugen *Acquittal*
Wo., Mathaeus *Acquittal*
Country where the crime was committed: Poland, Belarus
Crime Location: Bialystok, Bobruisk, Mogilew, unknown (marsh area to the south of Baranowicze), Cholm
Agency: Police Battalion 316
Subject of the proceedings: Mass shootings of Jews, partisans and their supporters, and of other persons, during the advance of the German Wehrmacht into Belorussia. Shooting of Jews employed in the removal of mass graves within the context of the so-called *Aktion 1005* in Cholm.

Case number: 690
Volume: XXX
Pages: 257–392

Court decision(s):
District Court Frankfurt/M., 19 August 1968
Federal High Court of Justice, 16 February 1971
Defendants:
Hahn, Fritz-Gebhardt von *8 Years*
Country where the crime was committed: Germany
Crime Location: Berlin
Agency: Ministry of Foreign Affairs
Subject of the proceedings: Cooperation in the deportation of Jews from Thracia and Macedonia to Auschwitz and Treblinka by the dispatchment of the SS-Hauptsturmführer Dannecker und Wisliceny as 'Jewish experts' to the German diplomatic corps in Sofia and Saloniki.

Case number: 697
Volume: XXXI
Pages: 407–478
Court decision(s):
District Court Frankfurt/M., 20 December 1968
Federal High Court of Justice, 27 October 1972
Defendants:
Allers, August Eduard Ernst Dietrich *8 Years*
Vorberg, Reinhold Paul Karl Robert *10 Years*
Country where the crime was committed: Germany
Crime Location: Berlin
Agency: Führer Chancellery (*Euthanasie-Aktion*)
Subject of the proceedings: Organizing and leading the 'Charitable Foundation for the Transport of Patients, Inc.', responsible for the transport of mentally ill patients to the extermination institutions and management of the central office 'T4'. Participation in the killing of concentration camp prisoners, who were crippled or unable to work, within the context of the so-called Special Treatment Operation '14f13'.

Case number: 733
Volume: XXIV
Pages: 187–294
Court decision(s):
District Court Frankfurt/M., 7 May 1970

Defendants:
Becker, Hans-Joachim *10 Years*
Lorent, Friedrich Wilhelm Siegmund Robert *7 Years*
Country where the crime was committed: Germany
Crime Location: Berlin
Agency: Führer Chancellery (*Euthanasie-Aktion*)
Subject of the proceedings: Cooperation, as leading officials of the T4-organization, in the killing of mentally ill patients, foreign workers and Jews, within the context of the *Euthanasie-Aktion* as well as of concentration camp prisoners who were disabled or otherwise unfit for work, within the context of the so-called Special Treatment Operation '14f13'.

Case number: 739
Volume: XXXIV
Pages: 577–641
Court decision(s):
District Court Karlsruhe, 23 September 1970
District Court Baden-Baden, 30 June 1967
Federal High Court of Justice, 15 August 1969
Defendants:
Reinhard, Hellmuth (alias Patzschke, Hellmuth) *5 Years*
Country where the crime was committed: Norway
Crime Location: Oslo
Agency: Gestapo Norway
Subject of the proceedings: Deportation of 532 Norwegian Jews to concentration camp Auschwitz. Ordering to kill Norwegian civilians in Oslo and Drammen as reprisal for acts of sabotage by the Norwegian resistance (*Aktion 'Blümchenpflücken'* – 'Flower picking'). Shooting of a civilian in Hokksund during a house search.

Case number: 745
Volume: XXXIV
Pages: 705–730
Court decision(s):
District Court Berlin 17 December 1970
Defendants:
Hartmann, Richard Eduard *6 Years*

Country where the crime was committed: Germany, France, Greece
Crime Location: Berlin, Cannes, Paris, Athens
Agency: RSHA Department IVB4 – 'Central Office for Jewish Resettlement'
Subject of the proceedings: Denying of emigration permits for, and furtherance of the deportation of Jews from Germany, France, Greece, Croatia and the Netherlands.

Case number: 746
Volume: XXXIV
Pages: 731–833
Court decision(s):
District Court Düsseldorf 22 December 1970
Defendants:
Stangl, Franz *Life sentence (died before sentence became final)*
Country where the crime was committed: Poland
Crime Location: Treblinka, Sobibor
Agency: Detainment Center Staff Treblinka/Sobibor
Subject of the proceedings: Supervision – as camp commander of Treblinka – of the mass extermination of at least 400.000 Jews and Gypsies. Shooting and hanging of Jews as well as supervision over the selections at the arrival ramp in Sobibor

Case number: 753
Volume: XXXV
Pages: 257–317
Court decision(s):
District Court Berlin, 6 April 1971
District Court Berlin, 13 October 1969
Federal High Court of Justice, 29 September 1970
Defendants:
Wöhrn, Fritz Oskar Karl *12 Years*
Country where the crime was committed: Germany
Crime Location: Berlin
Agency: RSHA Department IVb4 – 'Central Office for Jewish Resettlement'
Subject of the proceedings: Sending of several thousands of Jews to concentration camps on trivial grounds by means of protective custody orders (*Schutzhaftbefehlen*), forbidding the issuance of foreign (protection)

passports to Jews living in the Netherlands and deportation of Turkish Jews from the Netherlands to concentration camp.

Case number: 770
Volume: XXXVII
Pages: 109–139
Court decision(s):
District Court Hamburg, 24 March 1972
Defendants:
Bec., Anton *no punishment imposed*
Country where the crime was committed: Poland
Crime Location: Jozefow, Lomazy
Agency: Police Battalion 101 (Police Regiment 25)
Subject of the proceedings: Mass shooting of at least 1800 Jews within the context of the so-called *Aktion Reinhard*.

Case number: 771
Volume: XXXVII
Pages: 141–174
Court decision(s):
District Court Berlin, 11 April 1972
Defendants:
Bosshammer, Friedrich Robert *Life Sentence (died before judgment became final)*
Country where the crime was committed: Germany, Italy
Crime Location: Berlin, Verona, Padua
Agency: RSHA Department IVb4 – 'Central Office for Jewish Resettlement', Security Police Italy, Gestapo Padua
Subject of the proceedings: Participation in the deportation of German and foreign Jews to concentration camps as Gestapo official of the Jewish referat of the Main Security Head Office (RSHA), as Jewish expert with the Commander of the Security Police (BdS) Italy and as head of the Gestapo branch office in Padua

Case number: 772
Volume: XXXVII
Pages: 175–197

Court decision(s):
District Court Hamburg, 24 April 1972
Federal High Court of Justice, 13 March 1973
Defendants:
Bec., Heinrich Theodor *no punishment imposed*
Dre., Kurt *3 ½ Years (died before sentence became final)*
Hof., Wolfgang Hermann Robert *4 Years*
Country where the crime was committed: Poland
Crime Location: Jozefow, Lomazy, Konskowola
Agency: Police Battalion 101 (Police Regiment 25)
Subject of the proceedings: Mass and single killings of at least 2500 Jews within the context of the so-called *Aktion Reinhard*.

Case number: 774
Volume: XXXVII
Pages: 247–293
Court decision(s):
District Court Frankfurt/M. 6 June 197
Federal High Court of Justice 20 March 1974
Defendants:
Borm, Dr.med. Kurt Walter Werner *Acquittal*
Country where the crime was committed: Germany
Crime Location: Treblinka, Sobibor
Agency: Medical staff mental institutions Sonnenstein and Bernburg
Subject of the proceedings: Participation in the killing of mentally ill patients as assistant-physician

Case number: 830
Volume: XL
Pages: 819–877
Court decision(s):
District Court Hamburg, 9 March 1976
Federal High Court of Justice, 23 February 1978
Federal Constitutional Court, 16 April 1980
Defendants:
Aig., Josef *2 Years*
Eic., Wilhelm *12 Years*

Country where the crime was committed: Belarus
Crime Location: Forced Labor Camp Bobruisk
Agency: Waffen-SS Supply Center *Russland-Mitte*
Subject of the proceedings: Shooting of at least 50 Jews in the forest camp near Bobruisk.

Case number: 858
Volume: XLIII
Pages: 283–435
Court decision(s):
District Court Cologne, 11 February 1980
Defendants:
Hagen, Herbert Martin *12 Years*
Heinrichsohn, Ernst *6 Years*
Lischka, Kurt *10 Years*
Country where the crime was committed: France
Crime Location: Paris, Bordeaux
Agency: Security Police France, Security Police Bordeaux
Subject of the proceedings: Organizing the disenfranchisement and detainment of the Jews living in France as well as organizing their deportation to the concentration camps Auschwitz, Majdanek and to the extermination camp Sobibor.

Case number: 870
Volume: XLIV
Pages: 583–645
Court decision(s):
District Court Kiel, 8 July 1981
Defendants:
Asche, Kurt Heinrich *7 Years*
Country where the crime was committed: Belgium
Crime Location: Brussels
Agency: Security Police Brussels
Subject of the proceedings: Organizing the disenfranchisement and the arrest of Jews living in Belgium as well as their deportation to Auschwitz, Bergen-Belsen and Theresienstadt.

Case number: 875
Volume: XLV
Pages: 153–202
Court decision(s):
District Court Hamburg, 7 December 1981
Defendants:
Büs., Rolf Franz Robert *3½ Years*
Coe., Richard Emil Rudolph Carl von *2 Years*
Wig., Arpad Jakob Valentin *12½ Years*
Country where the crime was committed: Poland
Crime Location: Warsaw, Forced Labor Camp Treblinka
Agency: SS and Police Leader (SSPF) Warsaw, Gendarmerie Warsaw, Order police Warsaw
Subject of the proceedings: Passing on orders – among them the so-called Shooting Order – by the SSPF Warsaw, the deputy commander of the Gendarmerie and the intelligence officer in the staff of the commander of the Order police in Warsaw, to shoot Jews for violations without trials. At least 2300 Jews were shot on the basis of these orders. Shooting of at least 110 Jewish prisoners from the Treblinka labor camp ('T1') who were unfit for work.

Case number: 897
Volume: XLVI
Pages: 539–805
Court decision(s):
District Court Hagen, 4 October 1985
Defendants:
Frenzel, Karl August Wilhelm *Life Sentence*
Country where the crime was committed: Poland
Crime Location: Sobibor
Agency: Detainment Center Staff Sobibor
Subject of the proceedings: Mass gassings and single killings of at least 150.000 Jews (revision trial – see case number 642)

Case number: 904
Volume: XLVII
Pages: 535–567

Court decision(s):
District Court Bonn, 17 November 1988
Federal High Court of Justice, 30 November 1990
Defendants:
Korff, Modest Alfred Leonhard Graf von *Acquittal*
Country where the crime was committed: France
Crime Location: Chalons-sur-Marne
Agency: Security Police Chalons-sur-Marne
Subject of the proceedings: Participation in the deportation of Jews from the domain of the Security Police branch office Chalons-sur-Marne by ordering their arrest and transfer to detention camp Drancy, from where they were deported to Auschwitz.

Case number: 1176
Volume: IV (DDR-JuNSV)
Pages: 577–585
Court decision(s):
District Court Magdeburg, 20 February 1952
Defendants:
Hegener, Richard von *Life Sentence*
Ste., Walter *10 Years*
Country where the crime was committed: Germany
Crime Location: Berlin, Brandenburg, unknown (various locations)
Agency: Führer Chancellery, Charitable Foundation for the Transport of Patients, Inc. (*Euthanasie-Aktion*)
Subject of the proceedings: Participation in the organization and implementation of the *Euthanasie-Aktion* as leading official of the Führer Chancellery and deputy manager of the so-called Reich Committee for the Scientific Registration of Serious Hereditary and Constitutional Diseases (von Hegener). Transport of about 8000 patients to the Brandenburg penitentiary and/or to mental institutions and nursing homes where they were gassed (Ste.).

Notes

Preface

1. *Trials of War Criminals before the Nuremberg Military Tribunals (NMT)*, Nuremberg October 1946 – October 1949. XV vols, vol. IV, 'The Einsatzgruppen Case', 'Case No. 9' (United States of America vs. Otto Ohlendorf et al.).
2. *Justiz und NS-Verbrechen. Sammlung deutscher Strafurteile wegen nationalsozialistischer Tötungsverbrechen (JuNSV)*. Between 1968 and 1982, 22 volumes were published, containing the post-war judgments covering the years 1945 up to and including 1965. From 1996 until 2012 an additional 26 volumes were published with the judgments from the following years. Also, Rüter had in the meantime started to collect the East German trial judgments, which were published in a 14 volume set, entitled *DDR-Justiz und NS-Verbrechen. Sammlung ostdeutscher Strafurteile wegen nationalsozialistischer Tötungsverbrechen* (DDR-JuNSV). For more information on the project, including an overview of the criminal cases involved, see: www.expostfacto.nl.
3. Indeed, even to date, Christopher Browning's case study of the members of Police Battalion 101 still stands out as the best and most balanced example of a historian's use of this material for such an investigation. Christopher R. Browning, *Ordinary Men. Reserve Police Battalion 101 and the Final Solution in Poland* (New York: HarperCollins Publishers, 1992).
4. Cited in Michael Marrus, *The Holocaust in history* (Toronto: Lester & Orpen Dennys, 1987), 203.
5. Another – exceptionally fierce – opponent to such efforts was the French film-maker Claude Lanzmann. A highly illustrative example of this fierceness can be found in Ron Rosenbaum, *Explaining Hitler. The search for the origins of his evil* (New York: HarperPerennial, 1999), 251–276.
6. The citation stems from M. S. Arnoni, 'Het exemplaar van een soort', in M. S. Arnoni, *Niemand wil vrijheid. Essays* (Amsterdam: SUA, 1983), 11–15.

I. The Veiled Image

1. *"... besonders jetzt tu Deine Pflicht!" Briefe von Antifaschisten geschrieben vor ihrer Hinrichtung* (Berlin-Potsdam: VVN-Verlag, 1949), 73–75.
2. Danuta Czech, *Kalendarium der Ereignisse im Konzentrationslager Auschwitz-Birkenau 1939–1945* (Reinbek bei Hamburg: Rowohlt Verlag. 1989), 536. Lustiger, Arno, ed., *The Black Book of Polish Jewry. An Account of the Martyrdom of Polish Jewry under the Nazi Occupation* (Bodenheim: Syndikat Buchgesellschaft, 1995; photostatic reprint, originally published New York 1943), 97. Also: Wolfgang Benz, ed., *Dimension des Völkermords. Die Zahl der jüdischen Opfer des Nationalsozialismus* (München: R. Oldenbourg Verlag,

1991), 419. For an SS report on the annihilation of the Jews in Galicia, see Doc. 018-L ('Katzmann-report', 30 June 1943) in: *Trial of the Major War Criminals before the International Military Tribunal, Nuremberg, 14 November 1945 - 1 October 1946*, (Nuremberg: IMT, 1947–1949), vol. XXXVII, 391–410.
3. Abraham I. Katsh, ed., *Scroll of Agony. The Warsaw Diary of Chaim I. Kaplan* (London: Hamish Hamilton, 1966), 264, 268. For similar observations: Abraham Lewin, *A Cup of Tears. A Diary of the Warsaw Ghetto* (Antony Polonsky ed., Oxford: Basil Blackwell, 1988), 81; Oskar Rosenfeld, *Wozu noch Welt. Aufzeichnungen aus dem Getto Lodz*. Hanno Loewy ed. (Frankfurt am Main: Verlag Neue Kritik, 1994), 149; Hanno Loewy and Andrzej Bodek, eds, *'Les Vrais Riches'- Notizen am Rand. Ein Tagebuch aus dem Ghetto Lodz (Mai bis August 1944)* (Leipzig: Reclam Verlag, 1997), 64–65.
4. Katsh, *Scroll of Agony*, 264.
5. Dan Diner, ed., *Zivilisationsbruch. Denken nach Auschwitz* (Frankfurt am Main: Fischer Taschenbuch Verlag, 1988), 7. Yehuda Bauer, *American Jewry and the Holocaust. The American Jewish Joint Distribution Committee 1939 – 1945* (Detroit: Wayne State University Press, 1982), 187 – 189. For reactions elsewhere, see Walter Laqueur, *The Terrible Secret. Suppression of the Truth about Hitler's "Final Solution"* (Harmondsworth: Penguin Books, 1982); Bernard Wasserstein, *Britain and the Jews of Europe 1939–1945*, Oxford 1979.
6. Iain Hamilton, *Koestler. A Biography* (London: Secker & Warburg, 1982), 79. Arthur Koestler, *Bricks to Babel. A selection from 50 years of his writings, chosen and with new commentary by the author* (New York: Random House, 1980), 221–222. Reprinted by permission of Peters Fraser & Dunlop (www.petersfraserdunlop.com) on behalf of the Estate of Arthur Koestler.
7. Arthur Koestler, *The Yogi and the Commissar and other essays* (London: Hutchinson & Co., 1983; first published in 1945), 89–93. Koestler, *Bricks to Babel*, 231. Reprinted by permission of Peters Fraser & Dunlop (www.petersfraserdunlop.com) on behalf of the Estate of Arthur Koestler.
8. Abraham Lewin, *A Cup of Tears*, 81.
9. *IMT*, vol. XI, 414–415; Doc. 3868-PS, *IMT* vol. XXXIII, 275–276. Höss' response to the question whether he had ever felt sorry for the victims remained limited to *'Jawohl.'* Ibid., 401. For his later adjustment of the numbers of murdered victims, see G.M. Gilbert, *Nürnberger Tagebuch* (Frankfurt am Main: Fischer Bücherei, 1962), 448–450.
10. *IMT* vol. IV, 371. A slightly similar story was told by Dr. Wilhelm Höttl of the Reichssicherheitshauptamt in his deposition before the Nuremberg judges on November 26, 1945. In it Höttl described a conversation with Eichmann in August 1944, in which the latter allegedly remarked that he had become convinced that Germany would lose the war and that there would be no future for him personally as he was regarded as one of the most wanted war criminals, since he had been responsible for the deaths of millions of Jews. *IMT* vol. XXXI, Document 2738-PS, 85–87. For Eichmann's reactions to the depositions of Wisliceny and Höttl, see Jochen von Lang, ed., *Das Eichmann-Protokoll*.

Tonbandaufzeichnungen der israelischen Verhöre (Frankfurt am Main-Berlin-Vienna: Ullstein Buch, 1985), 106–107 and 150–151, and especially also his memoirs, published under the title *Ich, Adolf Eichmann. Ein historischer Zeugenbericht* by Dr. Rudolf Aschenauer (Leoni am Starnberger See: Druffel-Verlag, 1981), 460–461, 469–478 and 493–495.

11. Marrus, *The Holocaust in history*, 46. See also: Hans Mommsen, 'The realization of the unthinkable: the "Final Solution of the Jewish Question" in the Third Reich', in Gerhard Hirschfeld (ed.), *The policies of genocide: Jews and Soviet prisoners of war in Nazi Germany* (London, Boston, Sydney 1986), 97–144.
12. *IMT* vol. IV, 494.
13. Von dem Bach was sentenced to four years and ten months in 1961 by a German court for his role in the so-called *Röhm-Aktion*. The next year he received a life sentence for the murder of three Communists in 1933. Bach was never tried for his role in the mass murders. Ernst Klee, *Das Personenlexikon zum Dritten Reich. Wer war was vor und nach 1945* (Frankfurt am Main: S. Fischer Verlag, 2003), 23. On November, 23 1942, Bach noted in his diary: 'Certainly, the killing of women and children is a crime. If one can avoid it, one must. But one shouldn't believe everything that enemy propaganda claims, if one is familiar with their lies from 1914 to 1918. Anyhow, this sadism of individual persons is horrific. My conscience has, in any case, remained clear, because I have always maintained the humane option, even when I must hate.' Cited in the trial judgment of the District Court of Bochum of 5 June 1968, in: *JuNSV* vol. XXIX, 83 (case no. 678).
14. E. A. Cohen, *Het Duitse concentratiekamp; een medische en psychologische studie* (Amsterdam: H.J. Paris, 1952). (English translation appeared in 1953 under the title: *Human behavior in the concentration camp*, with W.W. Norton in New York). See also Willem Mooijman, Levensbericht van Elie Aron Cohen, *Jaarboek van de Maatschappij der Nederlandse Letterkunde* 1996, 73–80 (http://www.dbnl.org).
15. Cohen, *Het Duitse Concentratiekamp*, 193, 197. (Italics added, DdM.).
16. Lucy S. Dawidowicz, *The War against the Jews 1933 – 1945* (Toronto – New York – London – Sydney: Bantam Books, 1975), 221–223.
17. Daniel Jonah Goldhagen, *Hitler's Willing Executioners. Ordinary Germans and the Holocaust* (New York: Alfred A. Knopf, 1996), 394.
18. A comparison between the quotes from the authors just cited, with Hitler's, Goebbels' or Streicher's opinions on the subject, will make this clear very quickly. For examples of such 'parallel formulations', c.f. Adolf Hitler, *Mein Kampf* (München 1935), 69–70, 334–335 and 358; Werner Maser, *Adolf Hitler: Mein Kampf. Geschichte, Auszüge, Kommentare* (München: Moewig, 1983), 223–253; Henry Friedlander, 'The Manipulation of Language', in: Henry Friedlander and Sybil Milton, eds, *The Holocaust: Ideology, Bureaucracy and Genocide* (New York: Kraus International, 1980), 107.
19. On Müller and Huber (including the citations given here) see: Robert Gellately, *The Gestapo and the German society. Enforcing Racial Policy 1933–1945*

(Oxford: Clarendon Press, 1990), 50–57 (See also his observations on 'career policemen' such as Müller and Huber, 60). Robert Wistrich, *Wer war Wer im Dritten Reich. Ein biographisches Lexikon* (Frankfurt am Main: Fischer Taschenbuch Verlag, 1987), 246–247. Heinz Höhne, *Der Orden unter dem Totenkopf. Die Geschichte der SS* (München: Gondrom Verlag, 1990), 166–168. Edward Crankshaw, *Gestapo. Instrument of Tyranny* (London 1990), 96–98.

20. Interesting in this respect are the remarks by Von dem Bach in his discussions with the American psychiatrist in Nuremberg, Leo Alexander. Bach stressed that, upon entering the Soviet territories with his troops, he clearly recognized that he had been *fooled* by the anti-Semitic propaganda, as the Jewish population he was supposed to exterminate constituted no threat to the Germans at all. This recognition, however, did not stop him from continuing the killings. Leo Alexander, 'War Crimes and their Motivation: The Socio-Psychological Aspects', *Journal of Criminal Law and Criminology* 39/3 (1948), 309–318. For slightly similar comments from Auschwitz camp commander Rudolf Höss, see Martin Broszat, ed., *Kommandant in Auschwitz. Autobiographische Aufzeichnungen des Rudolf Höss* (München: Deutscher Taschenbuch Verlag, 1983), 152–153.
21. For the citations below, c.f. Ohlendorf Document Nr. 38, *NMT* Vol. IV 339–355 and 462–470.
22. Italics added, DdM.
23. *NMT*, Vol. IV, 587–589.
24. Comer Clarke, *De harde waarheid over Adolf Eichmann*, (Amsterdam-Maastricht: H.J.W. Becht, 1960), 7. Dutch translation of Clarke's *Eichmann: The Savage Truth* (London: World Distributors, 1960).
25. Harry Mulisch, *De zaak 40/61. Een reportage* (Amsterdam: Uitgeverij de Bezige Bij, 1964; first published 1961), 13–14.
26. Abel Herzberg, *Eichmann in Jeruzalem* (Den Haag: Bert Bakker, 1962), 10.
27. Hannah Arendt, *Eichmann in Jerusalem: A Report on the Banality of Evil* (Harmondsworth: Penguin Group, 1983), 48 and 54–55.
28. Among the many (German) books and articles addressing the subject, see, for example, Kerstin Freudiger, *Die juristische Aufarbeitung von NS-Verbrechen*. Tübingen 2002, and Jörg Friedrich, *Die kalte Amnestie. NS-Täter in der Bundesrepublik*. München 1994.
29. Apart from the information contained in the various trial judgments there exists an enormous amount of – mostly German – secondary literature on the subject. In English, the most comprehensive treatment is by Henry Friedlander, *The Origins of Nazi Genocide. From Euthanasia to the Final Solution* (Chapel Hill & London: The University of North Carolina Press, 1995).
30. Gitta Sereny, *Into that darkness. An examination of conscience* (London: Pan Books, 1977), 79. Dietrich Allers was tried and, on 20 December 1968, convicted by the District Court of Frankfurt am Main to eight years' imprisonment for his involvement in the 'mercy killing' program. The trial judgment is included in *JuNSV*, vol. XXXI, 408–465 (Case No. 697).

31. Allers' predecessor was Gerhard Bohne. On him, cf. Ernst Klee, *Was sie taten – was sie wurden. Ärzte, Juristen und andere Beteiligte am Kranken- oder Judenmord*. (Frankfurt am Main: Fischer Taschenbuch Verlag, 1986), 29–33.
32. Aller's wife confirmed his impression and added that she herself also got into T4 with the help of a friend. Sereny, *Into that Darkness*, 80.
33. In the same trial as Allers, Reinhold Vorberg was sentenced to ten years for his role in the T4 operation. *JuNSV*, vol. XXXI, 408–465 (Case No. 697). For Gerhart Siebert, see Klee, *Was sie taten*, 67, 82 and 295 note 111; Hans-Joachim Becker was tried before the District Court of Frankfurt am Main in 1970. He was sentenced to ten years' imprisonment. *JuNSV*, vol. XXXIV, 188–290 (Case No. 733). Herbert Linden committed suicide in Berlin, in April 1945. Ernst Klee, *Das Personenlexikon zum Dritten Reich. Wer war was vor und nach 1945* (Frankfurt am Main 2003), 373.
34. Friedrich Lorent was tried alongside Becker by the Frankfurt court and received a seven years' sentence. For the family-ties between Willy Schneider and Alfred Ittner, see the trial judgment of the District Court of Hagen of 20 December 1966 (which sentenced Ittner to four years for his role in the Sobibor extermination camp), in: *JuNSV*, Bd. XXV, 164 (Case No. 642). For Fritz Schmiedel, see Klee, *Was sie taten*, 81. For a comprehensive treatment of the various Aktion Reinhard trials in English, see Michael S. Bryant, *Eyewitness to Genocide. The Operation Reinhard Death Camp Trials, 1955–1966*. Knoxville 2014.
35. Franz Rum was sentenced to three years' imprisonment by the District Court of Düsseldorf for his role in the extermination camp of Treblinka. He died before his verdict became final. *JuNSV* vol. XXII, 2–220 (Case No. 596). Richard von Hegener was sentenced to life imprisonment by the District Court of Magdeburg on 20 February 1952. He was released in 1956 and settled in West Germany. *DDR-JuNSV* vol. IV, 579–585 (Case No. 1176); Klee, *Personenlexikon*, 237.
36. Josef Wolf was killed during the Sobibor revolt, in October 1943. His brother, Franz, was sentenced to eight years' imprisonment for his role in the Sobibor camp by the District Court of Hagen on 20 December 1966. *JuNSV* vol. XXV, 54–233 (Case No. 642). For the recruitment of the Wolf brothers by Franz Wagner, see 153. Suchomel was sentenced to six years' imprisonment by the District Court of Düsseldorf on 3 September 1965 for his role in Treblinka. *JuNSV* vol. XXII, 2–220 (Case No. 596). For Suchomel's recruitment, see Allers' comments in Sereny, *Into that Darkness*, 80.
37. Stangl was sentenced to life imprisonment by the District Court of Düsseldorf on 22 December 1970 for his role as camp commander of Treblinka. He died before his verdict became final. *JuNSV* vol. XXXIV, 732–833 (Case No. 746). For Stangl, see also Sereny, *Into that Darkness*, passim.
38. Eberhard Jäckel and Jürgen Rohwer, eds, *Der Mord an den Juden im Zweiten Weltkrieg. Entschlussbildung und Verwirklichung* (Stuttgart: Deutsche Verlags-Anstalt, 1985), 161.
39. See the judgment of the District Court Frankfurt am Main of 21 March 1947, in: *JuNSV* vol. I, 323–324 (Case No. 017).

40. For his role in the Treblinka murders Miete was sentenced to life imprisonment by the District Court of Düsseldorf, on 3 September 1965. *JuNSV* vol. XXII, 2–220 (Case No. 596).
41. Mentz was tried alongside Miete and also received a life sentence. Ibid.
42. Frenzel was sentenced to life imprisonment by the District Court of Hagen on 20 December 1966. His case was reopened before the same court in 1985 and resulted in the same sentence. JuNSV vol. XXV, 54–233 (Case No. 642) and vol. XLVI, 540–805 (Case No. 897).
43. *JuNSV* Bd. XXXI, 431 (Case No. 697).
44. At the time of their recruitment the NSDAP alone numbered some five million members. Michael H. Kater,., *The Nazi Party. A Social Profile of Members and Leaders, 1919–1945* (Cambridge, Harvard University Press, 1983), figure 1.
45. Sereny, *Into that Darkness*, 81.
46. Mitscherlich, Alexander and Fred Mielke, eds, *Medizin ohne Menschlichkeit. Dokumente des Nürnberger Ärzteprozesses* (Frankfurt am Main: Fischer Taschenbuch Verlag, 2012), 237. For earlier references by Hitler to the concept of medical killing, c.f. Klaus Dörner, 'Nationalsozialismus und Lebensvernichtung', *Vierteljahrshefte für Zeitgeschichte* 15 (1967–2), 131.
47. For the following (including the citations), see Lothar Gruchmann, *Justiz im Dritten Reich 1933–1940. Anpassung und Unterwerfung in der Ära Gürtner* (München 1988), 498–506.
48. For the full text of this memorandum, see Ernst Klee, ed., *Dokumente zur "Euthanasie"* (Frankfurt am Main: Fischer Taschenbuch Verlag, 1986), 151–162.
49. Gruchmann, *Justiz im Dritten Reich*, 506–507.
50. For this citation as well as the preceding ones, see Ibid., 506–508 and 514.
51. See the judgment of District Court of Frankfurt am Main of 6 June, 1972, in: *JuNSV*, vol. XXXVII, 266–267 (Case No. 774).
52. For an extensive treatment of Gürtner's character and position, see Gruchmann, *Justiz im Dritten Reich*, 9–83.
53. Ibid., 512; Klee, *Dokumente*, 204–207; *JuNSV*, vol. XXXI, 427 (Case No. 697).
54. Gruchmann, *Justiz im Dritten Reich*, 530.
55. Ernst Klee, *"Die SA Jesu Christi". Die Kirche im Banne Hitlers* (Frankfurt am Main: Fischer Taschenbuch Verlag, 1989), 85. (Italics added, DdM).
56. Judgment of the District Court of Frankfurt am Main of 27 May 1970, in: *JuNSV*, vol. XXXIV, 199 (Case No. 733).
57. Guenther Lewy. ' "Mit festem Schritt ins neue Reich." Die katholische Kirche zwischen Kreuz und Hakenkreuz', *Der Spiegel* (1965/15), 85–105. Eberhard Nitschke, 'Als es um das Kreuz ging, rebellierten die Oldenburger', *Die Welt*, 11-3-1988. For the position of the Churches towards the regime, see Martin Broszat, *Der Staat Hitlers. Grundlegung und Entwicklung seiner inneren Verfassung* (München: Deutscher Taschenbuch Verlag, 1983), 283–300 and Karl Dietrich Bracher, *Die deutsche Diktatur. Entstehung – Struktur – Folgen des Nationalsozialismus* (Frankfurt am Main: Ullstein, 1979), 411–423. Ulrich von Hehl, 'Die Kirchen in der NS-Diktatur. Zwischen Anpassung,

Selbstbehauptung und Widerstand', in: Karl Dietrich Bracher, Manfred Funke and Hans-Adolf Jacobsen, eds, *Deutschland 1933–1945. Neue Studien zur nationalsozialistischen Herrschaft* (Düsseldorf: Bundeszentrale für politische Bildung, 1993), 153–181.
58. Ernst Klee, *"Die SA Jesu Christi"*, passim; Idem, *Dokumente*, 143–198.
59. Ibid., 151.
60. On protests from church leaders, cf. Ernst Klee, *"Die SA Jesu Christi"*, 182–184 and the sources mentioned there. On Van Galen's sermon and its consequences, cf. Idem, *Dokumente*, 193–198; Idem, *"Euthanasie im NS-Staat." Die "Vernichtung lebensunwerten Lebens"* (Frankfurt am Main), 333–339. For the exact number of victims see the official T4 statistics as cited in *JuNSV*, Bd. XXXI, 429 (Case No. 697).
61. Cf., for example, the letter of 25 November 1940, sent by the head of the National Socialist Women's League, Else Löwis, to the wife of the Supreme Party Judge of the NSDAP, Walter Buch, on the 'mercy killing' practices. It is partially cited in Ibid. For an extended treatment of this letter, including its consequences, cf. Ernst Klee, *"Euthanasie im NS-Staat." Die "Vernichtung lebensunwerten Lebens"* (Frankfurt am Main: S. Fischer Verlag, 1983), 289–291.
62. For Frenzel, cf. *JuNSV*, vol. XXV, 117 (Case No. 642) and the report of his conversation with Toivi Blatt, in *Stern* of 22 March 1984: 'Der Mörder und sein Zeuge'; for Stangl, cf. Sereny, *Into that Darkness*, 37; for Wirth, cf. his personnel file listed as annex in Jochen von Lang, *Das Eichmann Protokoll. Tonbandaufzeichnungen der israelischen Verhöre* (Berlin 1982).
63. Klee, *"Die SA Jesu Christi."*, 167.
64. Cf. in this respect also the observations in Herbert Jäger, *Verbrechen unter totalitärer Herrschaft. Studien zur nationalsozialistischen Gewaltkriminalität* (Frankfurt am Main: Suhrkamp Taschenbuch, 1982), 174–175.
65. For the examples given here, cf. *JuNSV* vol. XXII, (Case No. 596), 48–49, 92, 97–98, 107–108, 120, 137–138, 151–152, 161–162, 164–165 and 168–169. In general, cf. also Klee, *Was sie taten*.
66. See also Sara Berger, *Experten der Vernichtung. Das T4-Reinhardt-Netzwerk in den Lagern Belzec, Sobibor und Treblinka* (Hamburg: Hamburger Edition, 2013), 363–364.
67. 'Zeig dich mit deinem Hund ....' *Rheinische Post* 5 February 1965.
68. For these and similar impressions, cf., for example, Heinz Schweden, 'Alle beschuldigen Franz', *Rheinische Post* 14 October 1964; Gerd Goch, 'Peitschenhiebe bis zum Massengrab', *Westdeutsche Allgemeine* 9 October 1964; Werner Diederichs, 'Sobibor ... was ist das?', *Ruhr-Nachrichten* 13 April 1966.
69. The most authoritative study on the subject still remains Adalbert Rückerl ed., *NS-Vernichtungslager im Spiegel deutscher Strafprozesse. Belzec, Sobibor, Treblinka, Chelmno* (München: Deutscher Taschenbuch Verlag, 1977). Including extensive references to the existing literature on the subject, see also: Berger, *Experten der Vernichtung*; Michael S. Bryant, *Eyewitness to Genocide.*

70. Cf. the quote from his diary entry on 2 September 1942, cited in the judgment against Kremer by the District Court of Münster of 29 November 1960, in: *JuNSV*, vol. XVII, 9 (Case No. 500).
71. Document 1919-PS, *IMT*, vol. XXIX, 145. In early February of the same year Himmler had visited Sobibor on an 'inspection tour.' Himmler witnessed the gassing of some 200 Jewish girls, who had been specifically selected for the occasion. The SS chief was impressed by the procedure, complimented the camp's staff on its work and promised them promotions and distinctions. *JuNSV*, vol. XLVI, 588, 621 and 698 (Case No. 897).
72. Simon Wiesenthal, *Moordenaars onder ons* (Amsterdam – Brussels: Elsevier, 1968), 135.
73. Mulisch, *De zaak 40/61*, 125. For similar observations, see Peter Krause, *Der Eichmann-Prozess in der deutschen Presse* (Frankfurt am Main: Campus Verlag, 2002), 166–190; Hans Lamm, ed., *Der Eichmann-Prozess in der deutschen öffentlichen Meinung* (Frankfurt am Main: Ner-Tamid-Verlag, 1961).
74. For obvious reasons much has been speculated on the nature of this secret OT mission. After all, it remains quite difficult to understand why these extermination experts were suddenly chosen to be involved in such a humanitarian task as the care for wounded soldiers. However, there exist no clues that the men who were included in this group did anything else than just that. In many of the trial judgments against members of the Aktion Reinhard staff, this mysterious mission is mentioned, but details on it are lacking. For a discussion of the mission, see Klee, *"Euthanasie"*, 372–373; Friedlander, *The origins of Nazi genocide*, 296–297.
75. Judgment by the District Court of Berlin of 8 May 1950, in: *JuNSV*, vol. VI, 545–560 (Case No. 212); Rückerl, *NS-Vernichtungslager*, 40. Bauer's death sentence was later commuted to life imprisonment. He was released on 22 December 1971 and died on 4 February 1980. *JuNSV*, vol. XLVI, 614 (Case No. 897).
76. *JuNSV*, vol. XXII, 56–58 (Case No. 596).
77. Rückerl, *NS-Vernichtungslager*, 295. See also the observations by Wolfgang Scheffler in his review of Hannah Arendt's *Eichmann in Jerusalem*, in *Aus Politik und Zeitgeschichte. Beilage zur Wochenzeitung Das Parlement* (B43/64, 21 November 1964), 36.

II. Pars pro Toto

1. *JuNSV*, vol. XXXIV, 732–833 (Case No. 746).
2. Gitta Sereny, *Into that darkness. An examination of conscience* (London 1977, Picador edition).
3. Ibid., 23 and 13, respectively.
4. Wiesenthal, *Moordenaars onder ons*, 336–337. See also 'Schwiegersohn lieferte KZ-Stangl aus' *Allgemeine Zeitung*, Mainz, 30 May 1970.
5. 'Mord hinter dem Guckloch' *Stern* 9 July 1967.

6. *JuNSV*, vol. XXXIV, 830 (Case No. 746). The *Lazarett* or 'hospital' was in fact an area within the camp where prisoners and deportees were executed by shooting and where their bodies were subsequently burned in large pits. See: Ibid., vol. XXII, 36 (Case No.596).
7. *Rheinische Post* 16 December 1970.
8. See, e.g., 'Hauptangeklagter Franz fordert Freispruch', *Die Welt* 25 August 1965; Werner Diederichs, 'Das letzte Wort der elf von Sobibor: ' "Sie werden keinen grausamen Zug in meinem Gesicht finden können"', *Essener Tageblatt* 13 December 1966.
9. Sereny, *Into that darkness*, 28.
10. Ibid., 31.
11. *JuNSV*, vol. XXXIV, 741 (Case No. 746).
12. Idem, 742. Stangl about Prohaska to Sereny: 'he hated my guts....' Sereny, *Into that darkness*, 37–38.
13. *JuNSV*, vol. XXXIV, 742–743 (Case No. 746); Sereny, *Into that darkness*, 32–33.
14. 'Was die Zeugin Stangl vor Gericht aussagte', *Leverkusener Anzeiger/Kölner Stadt-Anzeiger*, 10 June 1970; *JuNSV* vol. XXXIV, 742 (Case No. 746); Sereny, *Into that darkness*, 38.
15. *JuNSV*, vol. XXXIV, 744 and 821 (Case No. 746). Also Sereny, *Into that darkness*, 33 and 46–47.
16. Stefan Zweig, *Die Welt von Gestern. Erinnerungen eines Europäers* (Frankfurt am Main: Fischer Taschenbuch Verlag, 2013; originally published in Stockholm 1942), 428–429 and 456.
17. Within a couple of months, NSDAP membership surged from 850.000 to 2,5 million. These new 'proselytes' were treated with considerable suspicion. See Martin Broszat, *Der Staat Hitlers*, 43 and 252–253; Kater, *The Nazi Party*, (figure 1) and 73–115; Bernd Wegner, *Hitlers politische Soldaten: die Waffen-SS 1933–1945*, (Paderborn, 1983), 81 note 8.
18. Section 211 of the German Criminal Code reads: '(1) Whosoever commits murder under the conditions of this provision shall be liable to imprisonment for life. (2) A murderer under this provision is any person who kills a person for pleasure, for sexual gratification, out of greed or otherwise *base motives*, by stealth or cruelly or by means that pose a danger to the public or in order to facilitate or to cover up another offence.' Michael Bohlander (transl.), *German Criminal Code*, Saarbrücken 2009.
19. *JuNSV*, vol. XXXIV, 740 (Case No. 746). See also Sereny, *Into that darkness*, 35–36.
20. *JuNSV*, vol. XXXIV, 737 (Case No.746). Curiously enough, Sereny does not mention Reichleitner's role in Stangl's recruitment, even though it was brought up during his trial. How Reichleitner himself wound up with T4 remains unknown, but, as Allers suggested to Sereny, it appears likely that in both his and Stangl's recruitment, the Upper Danube district's Gauleiter in Linz, August Eigruber, was instrumental. Eigruber became deputy head of the nearby Hartheim extermination center, where Reichleitner and Stangl were employed

and he knew both men from the Linz Gestapo office. Sereny, *Into that darkness*, 81. On Eigruber, cf. Klee, *Personenlexikon*, 131.
21. For Stangl's recruitment with T4 and his tasks at Hartheim, see Sereny, *Into that darkness*, 48–56. Also: *JuNSV*, vol. XXXIV, 737–738 (Case No. 746).
22. According to the same statistician, the total number of patients gassed in Hartheim up to August 1941 numbered 18.269. Ibid., 230 (Case No. 733).
23. For the gassing of concentration camp prisoners and forced laborers, cf. the trial judgments of the District Court of Cologne of 30 October 1967, in Ibid., vol. XXVI, 568–820 (Case No.659), of the District Court of Hagen of 29 October 1968, in Ibid., vol. XXX, 414–687 (Case No.692), and of the District Court of Frankfurt am Main of 27 May 1970, in Ibid., vol. XXXIV, 188–294 (Case No. 733).
24. For the above, cf. Ibid., vol. XXXIV, 738 and 772 (Case No. 746), vol. XXV, 94 (Case No. 642); Sereny, *Into that darkness*, 78–79 and 113–114. For the Italian assignment, see Rückerl, *NS-Vernichtungslager*, 75; Klee, *Was sie taten*, 57–58 and 287, notes 5–9; Susan Zuccotti, *The Italians and the Holocaust. Persecution, Rescue & Survival* (London: Peter Halban, 1987), 184–186; Berger, *Experten der Vernichtung*, 278–291.
25. Cf., for example, Michael Burleigh, *Death and Deliverance.'Euthanasia' in Germany 1900–1945* (Cambridge: Cambridge University Press, 1994), 127 and Abram de Swaan, *The Killing Compartments. The Mentality of Mass Murder* (New Haven and London: Yale University Press, 2015), 15 and 36–37.
26. See Helge Grabitz, *NS-Prozesse. Psychogramme der Beteiligten* (Heidelberg, C.F. Müller Juristischer Verlag, 1986). And, especially with regard to the so-called Aktion Reinhard trials, the highly informative book by the former director of the Zentrale Stelle der Landesjustizverwaltungen (Federal Bureau for the Investigation of Nazi Crimes), Adalbert Rückerl, *NS-Vernichtungslager*.
27. Heiner Lichtenstein, *Im Namen des Volkes? Eine persönliche Bilanz der NS-Prozesse* (Köln: Bund-Verlag, 1984), 186–195; Rückerl, *NS-Vernichtungslager*, 78–79.
28. Ibid., 78.
29. Cf. the decisions of the District Court München I, 30 January 1964 and of the District Court of Appeal München, 22 July 1964.
30. *JuNSV* vol. XXII, 2–220 (Case No. 596). For its treatment of the Befehlsnotstand question cf. especially 198–210.
31. Every three months, the Treblinka staff members were entitled to two or three weeks' vacation, which, together with their wives, they could spend at the luxurious T4 rest home at the Attersee lake, near Salzburg. For the other 'benefits' of their Treblinka employment, see Ibid., 43–44.
32. Ibid., 207.
33. Ibid., 160.
34. Ibid., 212.
35. Judgment of the District Court of Hagen 20 December 1966, in: *JuNSV*, vol. XXV, Case No. 641/642, 16–233.

36. Adalbert Rückerl, *NS-Verbrechen vor Gericht. Versuch einer Vergangenheitsbewältigung* (Heidelberg: C.F. Müller Juristischer Verlag, 1984), 282–283; Ulrich Herbert, *Best. Biographische Studien über Radikalismus, Weltanschauung und Vernunft 1903–1989* (Bonn: J.H.W. Dietz, 2001), 495.
37. For examples, see also the following newspaper articles on the subject: 'Rudel schoss Akten in Brand', *Die Welt* 17 November 1964; 'Treueprämien für Euthanasie-Angestellte', *Frankfurter Allgemeine Zeitung* 17 November 1964; '"T4"-Stiftung schickte Wachmännern Rotwein', *Westfalenpost* 17 November 1964.
38. 'Wie ein roter Faden zieht sich dieses mit Ehrgeiz gepaarte Zweckmäßigkeits- und Nützlichkeitsdenken durch seinen ganzen Lebenslauf bis zu seiner erwähnten Beförderung in Treblinka. ... Das Denken und Handeln des Angeklagten entsprang seinem Streben nach eigenem Fortkommen um jeden Preis.' *JuNSV* vol. XXXIV, 821 (Case No. 746).
39. Ibid., 794.
40. Sereny, *Into that darkness*, 57–58.
41. Ibid., 169–170.
42. Ibid., 207–208.
43. *JuNSV*, vol. XXXIV, 831 (Case No.746); Ibid. vol. XXV, 223 (Case No.642).
44. Ibid., vol. XXII, 107–120 and 187–189 (Case No.596).
45. Cf. in this respect also Herbert Jäger's observations in *Verbrechen unter totalitärer Herrschaft*, 166–251.
46. For reactions to Franz's remarks, see 'Zuhörer protestieren laut' *Neue Rhein Zeitung* 20 October 1964. For the closing statements of the Treblinka trial defendants: 'Hauptangeklagter Franz fordert Freispruch' *Die Welt* 25 August 1965; *JuNSV*, vol. XXII, 55 (Case No. 596). For the closing statements of the Sobibor trial defendants: ' "Sie werden keinen grausamen Zug in meinem Gesicht finden können"' *Ruhr-Nachrichten* 13 December 1966.
47. Sereny, *Into that darkness*, 364.
48. Ibid., 366.
49. Ibid., 24.

III. The Palmström Syndrome

1. Adolf Hitler, *Mein Kampf* (München: Zentralverlag der NSDAP. Frz. Eher Nachf., 1935), 18; Joachim Fest, *Hitler. Eine Biographie* (Frankfurt am Main-Berlin-Wien: Ullstein Verlag, 1973), 2 vols, vol.I, 52; Paul Roazen, *Freud and his followers* (Harmondsworth: Penguin, 1973), 192.
2. Ron Rosenbaum, *Explaining Hitler*, 305–306.
3. Erich Fromm, *The Anatomy of Human Destructiveness* (New York – Chicago – San Francisco: Holt, Rinehart and Winston, 1973), 83–84.
4. See, however, Peter Gay, *Freud. A Life for Our Time* (New York: Anchor Books, 1989), 549–551.

5. Hannah Arendt, 'Organized Guilt and Universal Responsibility', in Ron H. Feldman, ed., *The Jew as Pariah. Jewish Identity and Politics in the Modern Age* (New York: Grove Press, 1978), 232 (Arendt's article was originally published in *Jewish Frontier* in January 1945). See also her similar observations in *The Origins of Totalitarianism* (San Diego – New York – London: Harcourt Brace Jovanovich, 1973), 338. With specific regard to the SS in Auschwitz, see Hermann Langbein, *Menschen in Auschwitz* (Wien: Europa Verlag, 1987), 315–316 and 319–320.
6. *JuNSV* vol. XLV, 197 (Case No. 875).
7. See, for example, the findings of the British *Parliamentary Commission on Banking Standards* of June 2013: www.parliament.uk/bankingstandards.
8. Joris Luyendijk, *Swimming with Sharks. Inside the World of the Bankers* (London: Guardian Books and Faber & Faber, 2016). For the citations below (italics added, DdM), cf. 245–246.
9. Ibid., 166. Compare this with the example given by Henry Friedlander of the Austrian worker Vinzenz Nohel, who, in 1939, had to support a family of six on a monthly income of a 100 Reichsmarks. Nohel was offered a job as a 'burner' in the crematoria of Hartheim against a salary of three times as much, as well as a daily ration of liquor. Henry Friedlander, *The Origins of Nazi Genocide*, 233–234.
10. *JuNSV*, vol. XXII, 163 (Case No. 596).
11. Gitta Sereny, *Albert Speer. His battle with truth* (London: Picador, 1996), 368.
12. Albert Speer, *Erinnerungen* (Frankfurt am Main – Berlin – Wien: Ullstein Verlag, 1982; originally published 1969), 385.
13. Ibid., 386.
14. For Speer's cautiousness when choosing his words, especially with regard to his 'confessions of guilt', see Sereny, *Speer*, 706–708 and Karl-Heinz Janssen, 'Die angebliche Entlarvung. Albert Speers wiederholt nur Allzubekanntes', *Die Zeit*, 1982/31.
15. In the spring of 1943, an incident took place on this same Obersalzberg which illustrates what would have happened to Speer if he had asked Hitler about Auschwitz. During an afternoon tea in the presence of Hitler, the wife of the Viennese Gauleiter and Reichstatthalter, Baldur von Schirach, mentioned a horrible scene she had witnessed in Amsterdam involving the deportation of Jews, and asked Hitler whether he approved of such measures. A painful silence followed, after which Hitler left the party without a comment. The Schirach couple were thereafter banned from the Berghof. Even though Speer denied having been present during the incident, he became aware of it shortly thereafter. See Traudl Junge, *Bis zur letzten Stunde. Hitlers Sekretärin erzählt ihr Leben* (München: List Taschenbuch, 2002), 100–101. Sereny, *Speer*, 111.
16. In September 1964, Wolff was sentenced to 15 years' imprisonment by the District Court of Munich II. For the trial judgment, see: *JuNSV* vol. XX, 380–504 (Case No. 580).
17. Ibid., 458.

18. Judgment of the District Court of Nürnberg-Fürth of 17 March 1952, in: *JuNSV*, vol. XXVIII, 126 (Case No.673). Rademacher was finally sentenced to 3 ½ years by the District Court of Bamberg in May 1968. Ibid., 23–111.
19. Judgment of the District Court of Frankfurt am Main of 19 August 1968, in: JuNSV, vol. XXX, Case No. 690, p. 347. Von Hahn was sentenced to 8 years.
20. Judgment of the District Court of Baden-Baden of 30 June 1967, in: JuNSV, vol. XXXIV, 607 (Case No.739). Reinhard was sentenced to 5 years.
21. Judgment of the District Court of Berlin of 17 December 1970, in: JuNSV, vol. XXXIV, 723–724 (Case No. 745). Hartmann was sentenced to 6 years.
22. Judgment of the District Court of Berlin of 13 October 1969, in: JuNSV, vol. XXXV, 298–299 (Case No.753). Wöhrn was sentenced to 12 years.
23. Judgment of the District Court Berlin of 11 April 1972, in: JuNSV, vol. XXXVII, 167 (Case No.771). Bosshammer died before his verdict became final.
24. Judgment of the District Court of Cologne of 11 February 1980, in: JuNSV, vol. XLIII, 388–389 (Case No. 858). Hagen was sentenced to 12 years; Lischka to 10 years and Heinrichsohn to 6 years.
25. Judgment of the District Court of Kiel of 8 July 1981, in: JuNSV vol. XLIV, 632 (Case No.870). Asche was sentenced to 7 years.
26. Judgment of the District Court of Bonn of 17 November 1988, in: JuNSV, vol. XLVII, 552 (Case No. 904). Von Korff was acquitted.
27. See Herbert, *Best*, 499–500.
28. See *JuNSV*, Bd. XXV, 394–651 (Case No. 645). For the citations below, see Christian Ritz, *Schreibtischtäter vor Gericht. Das Verfahren vor dem Münchner Landgericht wegen der Deportation der niederländischen Juden (1959–1967)* (Paderborn: Ferdinand Schöningh, 2012), 171–173; 'Harster und Zoepf wiederholen ihr Schuldbekenntnis', *Münchner Merkur* 18 February 1967.
29. 'Immer nur Richtlinien' *Abend-Zeitung*, München 28 January 1967. Italics added.
30. Browning, *Ordinary Men*, 189.
31. Jäger, *Verbrechen unter totalitärer Herrschaft*, 14. Jäger's book was originally published in 1967.
32. Bettina Stangneth, *Eichmann vor Jerusalem. Das unbehelligte Leben eines Massenmörders* (Zürich – Hamburg: Arche Literaur Verlag, 2011).
33. Cf. Eichmann's comments on Wisliceny's statement in his 'memoirs', in which he objects to being misquoted: he allegedly never mentioned 'Menschen' or 'Juden' but 'Reichsfeinde' ['enemies of the Reich']. Rudolf Aschenauer (Hrsg.), *Ich, Adolf Eichmann. Ein historischer Zeitzeugenbericht* (Augsburg 1981), 494–495.
34. *Aufzeichnungen von Avner W. Less, 23.5.-17.8.1960 betr. das Verhör mit Adolf Eichmann*, entry 16 June 1960. Eidgenössische Technische Hochschule Zürich (ETH), Archiv für Zeitgeschichte, Nachlass Less, Avner W.
35. Stangneth, *Eichmann*, 61.
36. De Swaan, *The Killing Compartments*, 22. For similar views, see Guenter Lewy, *Perpetrators. The World of the Holocaust Killers* (Oxford: Oxford University Press, 2017); David Cesarani, *Eichmann. His Life and Crimes* (London: Vintage

Books, 2005); Yaacov Lozowick, *Hitler's Bureaucrats. The Nazi Security Police and the Banality of Evil* (London – New York: Continuum, 2002).
37. Abram de Swaan, *Compartimenten van vernietiging. Over genocidale regimes en hun daders* (Amsterdam: Prometheus – Bert Bakker, 2014), 29.
38. Judgment of the District Court of Hamburg of 9 March 1976, in: *JuNSV*, vol. XL, 855–856 (Case No. 830).
39. De Swaan, *The Killing Compartments*, 37.
40. In this respect, see the opinions of the judges on the members of the police battalion to which De Swaan refers here: Judgments of the District Court of Hamburg of 8 April 1968, 24 March and 24 April 1972, respectively, in: *JuNSV*, vol. XXVII, 526–650 (Case No. 670), vol. XXXVII, 110–139 (Case No. 770), and 176–197 (Case No. 772).
41. De Swaan, *The Killing Compartments*, 37.
42. '"The Formidable Dr. Robinson": A Reply by Hannah Arendt', in: Ron H. Feldman (ed.), *Hannah Arendt. The Jews as Pariah. Jewish identity and Politics in the Modern Age* (New York 1978), 260–276. See also Ernst Simon, 'Hannah Arendt – Eine Analyse', in *Nach dem Eichmann Prozess. Zu einer Kontroverse über die Haltung der Juden* (Tel Aviv: Bitaon Publishing Co., 1963), 51–97.
43. Ibid., 273.
44. De Swaan, *The Killing Compartments*, 22.
45. For Servatius' arguments see: *Prozess vor dem Bezirksgericht Jerusalem, Sitzungsprotokolle Nr. 114*, 14.8.1961, ETH, Archiv für Zeitgeschichte, Nachlass Less, Avner W. For Eichmann's own views on his motives, see Arendt, *Eichmann*, 25 and 135–137. Cf. also Eichmann's own comments on the 'small cog theory': Cesarani, *Eichmann*, 312.
46. See, however, the complete acceptance of Hausner's version by the Appeal Court: Arendt, *Eichmann*, 249.
47. Ibid., 57–58, 126 and 289.
48. Ibid., 136–137. To this passage, Arendt adds a more general observation, which reads as follows: 'Much of the horribly painstaking thoroughness in the execution of the Final Solution – a thoroughness that usually strikes the observer as typically German, or else as characteristic of the perfect bureaucrat – can be traced to the odd notion, indeed very common in Germany, that to be law-abiding means not merely to obey the laws but to act as though one were the legislator of the laws that one obeys. Hence the conviction that *nothing less than going beyond the call of duty will do.*' Italics added, DdM.
49. Ibid., 138.
50. *Tonbandtranskription des Verhörs von Adolf Eichmann, geführt von Avner W. Less*, Mahane Iyar, 1960, Vol. No. 5, 32. ETH, Archiv für Zeitgeschichte, Nachlass Less, Avner W.
51. Ibid., 49.
52. *Aufzeichnungen von Avner W. Less, 23.5.-17.8.1960 betr. das Verhör mit Adolf Eichmann*, entry of 11 June 1960.

53. Stangneth, *Eichmann*, 625 (note 1165).
54. See the observations of Less in Jochen von Lang (Hrsg.), *Das Eichmann-Protokoll. Tonbandaufzeichnungen der israelischen Verhöre* (Berlin 1982), 267. Also: Arendt, *Eichmann*, 287.
55. In: Christian Morgenstern, *Palmström* (Berlin 1910).
56. For its relation to perpetrator behavior, see in particular: Leonard S. Newman, 'What is a "Social-Psychological" Account of Perpetrator Behavior? The Person versus the Situation in Goldhagen's *Hitler's Willing Executioners*', in Leonard S. Newman and Ralph Erber, eds, *Understanding Genocide. The Social Psychology of the Holocaust* (New York: Oxford University Press, 2002), 52–57.
57. Arendt, *Eichmann*, 287.
58. See Rolf Schroers, 'Der banale Eichmann und seine Opfer' in: F.A. Krummacher, ed., *Die Kontroverse. Hannah Arendt, Eichmann und die Juden* (München: Nymphenburger Verlagshandlung, 1964), 200. It is hardly a coincidence that De Swaan's discussion of Arendt's theses comes under the heading 'The Banalization of Evil', De Swaan, *The Killing Compartments*, 21.
59. Arendt, *Eichmann*, 276.
60. *Aufzeichnungen von Avner W. Less, 23.5.-17.8.1960 betr. das Verhör mit Adolf Eichmann*, entry of 11 June 1960, ETH, Archiv für Zeitgeschichte, Nachlass Less, Avner W.
61. Cf. in this respect also the observations of Rolf Schroers in Krummacher (Hrsg.), *Die Kontroverse*, 200–201.
62. De Swaan, *The Killing Compartments*, 264.
63. Cf. Arendt, *Eichmann*, 286.

Postscript
1. Alan Bullock, *Adolf Hitler. A Study in Tyranny* (London: Odhams, 1952).

Bibliography

Unpublished sources

Antrag auf Eröffnung der gerichtlichen Voruntersuchung im Ermittlungsverfahren gegen Schlegelberger u.a. Js 20/63 (GstA), 22 April 1965.

Einstellungsbeschluss LG München I, 30 January 1964.

Beschluss OLG München, 22 July 1964.

Eidgenössische Technische Hochschule Zürich (ETH), Archiv für Zeitgeschichte, Nachlass Less, Dokumentation zum Eichmann-Prozess, Voruntersuchung durch das Büro 06 der israelischen Polizei, Verhör, Persönliche Unterlagen von Avner W. Less, Aufzeichnungen von Avner W. Less, 23.5.-17.8.1960 betr. das Verhör mit Adolf Eichmann. Prozess vor dem Bezirksgericht Jerusalem, Sitzungsprotokolle 11.4.1961-15.12.1961. Tonbandtranskription des Verhörs von Adolf Eichmann, geführt von Avner W. Less, Mahane Iyar, 1960.

Published sources

Justiz und NS-Verbrechen. Sammlung deutscher Strafurteile wegen nationalsozialistischer Tötungsverbrechen 1945–2012 (JuNSV). C. F. Rüter/D. W. de Mildt, eds, (Amsterdam: Amsterdam University Press, 1968–2012), 49 volumes.

DDR-Justiz und NS-Verbrechen. Sammlung ostdeutscher Strafurteile wegen nationalsozialistischer Tötungsverbrechen 1945–1990. (DDR-JuNSV). C. F. Rüter, ed. (Amsterdam: Amsterdam University Press, 2002–2010), 14 volumes.

Trial of the Major War Criminals before the International Military Tribunal, Nuremberg, 14 November 1945-1 October 1946. 42 vols, (Nuremberg: IMT, 1947–1949).

Trials of War Criminals before the Nuremberg Military Tribunals (NMT), Nuremberg October 1946 – October 1949. 15 volumes.

United Nations War Crimes Commission (eds.), *Law Reports of Trials of War Criminals* (London: His Majesty's Stationery Office, 1949). 15 volumes.

Literature

Adam, Uwe D., *Judenpolitik im Dritten Reich* (Düsseldorf: Athenäum Verlag, 1979).

Adelson, Alan, ed., *The Diary of Dawid Sierakowiak. Five Notebooks from the Lodz Ghetto* (London: Bloomsbury, 1996).

Adler, Hans G., *Theresienstadt 1941–1945. Das Antlitz einer Zwangsgemeinschaft. Geschichte – Soziologie – Psychologie* (Tübingen: J.C.B. Mohr, 1960).

Adler, Hans G., ed., *Die Verheimlichte Wahrheit. Theresienstädter Dokumente* (Tübingen: J.C.B. Mohr, 1958).

Adler, Hans G., ed., *Der Verwaltete Mensch. Studien zur Deportation der Juden aus Deutschland* (Tübingen: J.C.B. Mohr, 1974).

Adler, Hans G., Hermann Langbein and Ella Lingens-Reiner, eds., *Auschwitz. Zeugnisse und Berichte* (Köln and Frankfurt am Main: Europäische Verlagsanstalt, 1979).

Aharoni, Zvi and Wilhelm Dietl, *Operation Eichmann. Pursuit and Capture* (London: Cassel & Co., 1999).

Alexander, Leo, 'War Crimes and their Motivation: The Socio-Psychological Aspects', *Journal of Criminal Law and Criminology* 39/3 (1948).

Allen, William S., *The Nazi Seizure of Power. The Experience of a Single German Town 1922–1945* (Harmondsworth: Penguin Group, 1989).

Arendt, Hannah, *The Origins of Totalitarianism* (San Diego – New York – London: Harcourt Brace Jovanovich, 1973).

Arendt, Hannah, 'Organized Guilt and Universal Responsibility', in Ron H. Feldman, ed., *The Jew as Pariah. Jewish Identity and Politics in the Modern Age* (New York: Grove Press, 1978).

Arendt, Hannah, *Eichmann in Jerusalem: A Report on the Banality of Evil* (Harmondsworth: Penguin Group, 1983).

Arnoni, M. S., *Moeder was niet huis voor haar begrafenis. Verslag van een reis door een verloren vaderland. Een overlevende van Auschwitz-Birkenau terug in Polen* (Amsterdam: De Bezige Bij, 1982).

Arnoni, M. S., 'Het exemplaar van een soort', in M. S. Arnoni, ed., *Niemand wil vrijheid. Essays* (Amsterdam: SUA, 1983), 11–15.

Arnsberg, Paul and Wolfgang Scheffler, 'Zu Hannah Arendts "Eichmann in Jerusalem"', *Aus Politik und Zeitgeschichte. Beilage zur Wochenzeitung Das Parlament* (B43/64, 21 November 1964).

Aschenauer, Rudolf, ed., *Ich, Adolf Eichmann. Ein historischer Zeugenbericht* (Leoni am Starnberger See: Druffel-Verlag, 1981).

Bauer, Yehuda and Nathan Rothenstreich, eds., *The Holocaust as Historical Experience* (New York: Holmes & Meier Publishers, 1981).

Bauer, Yehuda and Nathan Rothenstreich, eds., *American Jewry and the Holocaust. The American Jewish Joint Distribution Committee 1939 – 1945* (Detroit: Wayne State University Press, 1982).

Baum, Rainer C., *The Holocaust and the German Elite. Genocide and National Suicide in Germany, 1871–1945* (New Jersey: Rowman and Littlefield, 1981).

Bauman, Zygmunt, *Modernity and the Holocaust* (Cambridge: Polity Press, 2008).

Behnken, Klaus, ed., *Deutschland-Berichte der Sozialdemokratischen Partei Deutschlands (Sopade) 1934–1940*. 7 vols, (Frankfurt am Main: Verlag Petra Nettelbeck, 1980).

Benz, Wolfgang, ed., *Dimension des Völkermords. Die Zahl der jüdischen Opfer des Nationalsozialismus* (München: R. Oldenbourg Verlag, 1991).

"... besonders jetzt tu Deine Pflicht!" Briefe von Antifaschisten geschrieben vor ihrer Hinrichtung (Berlin-Potsdam: VVN-Verlag, 1949).

Berg, Mary, *The Diary of Mary Berg. Growing up in the Warsaw Ghetto* (London: Oneworld Publications, 2013).

Berger, Sara, *Experten der Vernichtung. Das T4-Reinhardt-Netzwerk in den Lagern Belzec, Sobibor und Treblinka* (Hamburg: Hamburger Edition, 2013).

Boberach, Heinz, ed., *Meldungen aus dem Reich. Die geheimen Lageberichte des Sicherheitsdienstes der SS 1939–1945* (Hersching: Manfred Pawlak Verlagsgesellschaft, 1984).

Bobroszycki, Lucjan, ed., *The Chronicle of the Lodz Ghetto 1941–1944* (New Haven and London: Yale University Press, 1984).

Bracher, Karl D., *Die deutsche Diktatur. Entstehung – Struktur – Folgen des Nationalsozialismus* (Frankfurt am Main: Ullstein, 1979).

Bracher, Karl Dietrich, Manfred Funke and Hans-Adolf Jacobsen, eds., *Deutschland 1933–1945. Neue Studien zur nationalsozialistischen Herrschaft* (Düsseldorf: Bundeszentrale für politische Bildung, 1993).

Broszat, Martin, ed., *Kommandant in Auschwitz. Autobiographische Aufzeichnungen des Rudolf Höss* (München: Deutscher Taschenbuch Verlag, 1983).

Broszat, Martin, ed., *Der Staat Hitlers. Grundlegung und Entwicklung seiner inneren Verfassung* (München: Deutscher Taschenbuch Verlag, 1983).

Broszat, Martin and Klaus Schwabe, eds., *Die deutschen Eliten und der Weg in den Zweiten Weltkrieg* (München: Verlag C.H. Beck, 1989).

Broszat, Martin, Klaus Schwabe and Elke Fröhlich, *Alltag und Widerstand. Bayern im Nationalsozialismus* (München: Piper Verlag, 1987).

Browning, Christopher R., *Ordinary Men. Reserve Police Battalion 101 and the Final Solution in Poland* (New York: Harper Collins Publishers, 1992).

Browning, Christopher R., *The Path to Genocide. Essays on Launching the Final Solution* (Cambridge: Cambridge University Press, 1992).

Browning, Christopher R., *The Origins of the Final Solution. The Evolution of Nazi Jewish Policy, September 1939 – March 1942* (Jerusalem: Yad Vashem, 2004).

Browning, Christopher R., *Remembering Survival. Inside a Nazi Slave-Labor Camp* (New York – London: W.W. Norton & Company, 2010).

Bryant, Michael S., *Confronting the "Good Death". Nazi Euthanasia on Trial, 1945–1953* (Boulder: University Press of Colorado, 2005).

Bryant, Michael S., *Eyewitness to Genocide. The Operation Reinhard Death Camp Trials, 1955–1966* (Knoxville: University of Tennessee Press, 2014).

Bullock, Alan, *Adolf Hitler a Study in Tyranny* (London: Odhams, 1952).

Burleigh, Michael, *Death and Deliverance.'Euthanasia' in Germany 1900–1945* (Cambridge: Cambridge University Press, 1994).

Camus, Albert, *Le mythe de Sisyphe* (Paris: Editions Gallimard, 1942).

Central Commission for Investigation of German Crimes in Poland, *German Crimes in Poland* (Warsaw: Central Commission for Investigation of German Crimes in Poland, 1946), volume I.

Cesarani, David, *Eichmann. His Life and Crimes* (London: Vintage Books, 2005).

Chalk, Frank and Kurt Jonassohn, *The History and Sociology of Genocide. Analyses and Case Studies.* (New Haven and London: Yale University Press, 1990).

Clarke, Comer, *Eichmann: The Savage Truth* (London: World Distributors, 1960).

Cohen, Elie A., *Het Duitse concentratiekamp; een medische en psychologische studie* (Amsterdam: H.J. Paris, 1952).

Cohen, Elie A., *De negentien treinen naar Sobibor* (Amsterdam and Brussels: Elsevier, 1979).

Cohn, Willy, *Kein Recht – nirgends. Breslauer Tagebücher 1933–1941. Eine Auswahl* (Bonn: Bundeszentrale für politische Bildung, 2009).

Comité des Délégations Juives, *Die Lage der Juden in Deutschland 1933. Das Schwarzbuch – Tatsachen und Dokumente*. Herausgegeben vom Comité des Délégations Juives (Paris 1934) (Frankfurt am Main – Berlin – Wien: Ullstein Verlag, 1983).

Czech, Danuta, *Kalendarium der Ereignisse im Konzentrationslager Auschwitz-Birkenau 1939–1945* (Reinbek bei Hamburg: Rowohlt Verlag. 1989).

Dawidowicz, Lucy S., *The War against the Jews 1933 – 1945* (Toronto – New York – London – Sydney: Bantam Books, 1975).

Diner, Dan, ed., *Zivilisationsbruch. Denken nach Auschwitz* (Frankfurt am Main: Fischer Taschenbuch Verlag, 1988).

Diner, Dan, ed., *Ist der Nationalsozialismus Geschichte? Zu Historisierung und Historikerstreit* (Frankfurt am Main: Fischer Taschenbuch Verlag, 1988).

Dörner, Klaus, 'Nationalsozialismus und Lebensvernichtung', *Vierteljahrshefte für Zeitgeschichte* 15/2 (1967), 121–152.

Earl, Hilary, *The Nuremberg SS-Einsatzgruppen Trial 1945–1948* (Cambridge: Cambridge University Press, 2009).

Fest, Joachim, *Hitler. Eine Biographie* 2 vols, (Frankfurt am Main – Berlin – Wien: Ullstein Verlag, 1973).

Feuchert, Sascha, Erwin Leibfried and Jörg Riecke, eds., *Die Chronik des Gettos Lodz/Litzmannstadt 1941–1944* 5 vols, (Göttingen: Wallstein Verlag, 2007).

Friedlander, Henry, *The Origins of Nazi Genocide. From Euthanasia to the Final Solution* (Chapel Hill and London: The University of North Carolina Press, 1995).

Friedlander, Henry and Sybil Milton, eds., *The Holocaust: Ideology, Bureaucracy and Genocide* (New York: Kraus International, 1980).

Fromm, Erich, *The Anatomy of Human Destructiveness* (New York – Chicago – San Francisco: Holt, Rinehart and Winston, 1973).

Fuchs, Thomas, ed., *Strafgesetzbuch für das Deutsche Reich vom 15. Mai 1871. Historisch-synoptische Edition 1871–2009* (Mannheim: lexetius.com, 2010).

Gay, Peter, *Freud. A Life for Our Time* (New York: Anchor Books, 1989).

Gedenkbuch des Bundesarchivs für die Opfer der nationalsozialistischen Judenverfolgung in Deutschland (1933–1945) (online: bundesarchiv.de/gedenkbuch).

Gellately, Robert, *The Gestapo and the German society. Enforcing Racial Policy 1933–1945* (Oxford: Clarendon Press, 1990).

Gilbert, Gilbert M., *Nürnberger Tagebuch* (Frankfurt am Main: Fischer Bücherei, 1962).

Gilbert, Martin, *The Holocaust. The Jewish tragedy* (Glasgow: Fontana/Collins, 1989).

Goldhagen, Daniel J., *Hitler's Willing Executioners. Ordinary Germans and the Holocaust* (New York: Alfred A. Knopf, 1996).

Gottwaldt, Alfred und Diana Schulle, *Die 'Judendeportationen' aus dem Deutschen Reich 1941–1945. Eine kommentierte Chronologie* (Wiesbaden, Marixverlag, 2005).

Grabitz, Helge, *NS-Prozesse. Psychogramme der Beteiligten* (Heidelberg, C.F. Müller Juristischer Verlag, 1986).

Grossman, Wassili und Ilja Ehrenburg (Hrsg.), *Das Schwarzbuch. Der Genozid an den sowjetischen Juden* (Reinbek bei Hamburg: Rowohlt Verlag, 1995).

Gruchmann, Lothar, *Justiz im Dritten Reich 1933–1940. Anpassung und Unterwerfung in der Ära Gürtner* (München: R. Oldenbourg Verlag, 1988).

Grunberger, Richard, *A social history of the Third Reich* (Harmondsworth: Penguin Books, 1979.

Gutman, Israel, ed., *Enzyklopädie des Holocaust. Die Verfolgung und Ermordung der europäischen Juden* 3 vols, (Tel Aviv: Argon, 1989).

Haffner, Sebastian, *Anmerkungen zu Hitler* (Hamburg: Fischer Verlag, 1981).

Haffner, Sebastian, *Geschichte eines Deutschen – Die Erinnerungen* (Stuttgart and München: Deutsche Verlags-Anstalt, 2000).

Hamilton, Iain, *Koestler. A Biography* (London: Secker & Warburg, 1982).

Hehl, Ulrich von, 'Die Kirchen in der NS-Diktatur. Zwischen Anpassung, Selbstbehauptung und Widerstand', in K. Dietrich Bracher, M. Funke and H.-A. Jacobsen, eds., *Deutschland 1933–1945. Neue Studien zur nationalsozialistischen Herrschaft* (Düsseldorf: Bundeszentrale für politische Bildung, 1993).

Heiber, Helmut, *Die Republik von Weimar* (München: Deutscher Taschenbuch Verlag, 1966).

Henkys, Reinhard, *Die nationalsozialistischen Gewaltverbrechen. Geschichte und Gericht* (Berlin: Kreuz-Verlag, 1964).

Herbert, Ulrich, *Best. Biographische Studien über Radikalismus, Weltanschauung und Vernunft 1903–1989* (Bonn: J.H.W. Dietz, 2001).

Herbert, Ulrich, *Geschichte Deutschlands im 20. Jahrhundert* (Bonn: Bundeszentrale für politische Bildung, 2014).

Herzberg, Abel, *Eichmann in Jeruzalem* (Den Haag: Bert Bakker, 1962).

Hilberg, Raul, *Sonderzüge nach Auschwitz* (Mainz: Dumjahn, 1981).

Hilberg, Raul, *The Destruction of the European Jews*. 3 vols, (New York and London: Holmes & Meier Publishers, 1985).

Hilberg, Raul, *Perpetrators Victims Bystanders. The Jewish Catastrophe 1933–1945* (New York: Harper Collins Publishers, 1992).

Hilberg, Raul, *The Politics of Memory. The Journey of a Holocaust Historian* (Chicago: Ivan R. Dee, 1996).

Hilberg, Raul, *Die Quellen des Holocaust. Entschlüsseln und Interpretieren* (Frankfurt am Main: Fischer Taschenbuch Verlag, 2009).

Hirschfeld, Gerhard, ed., *The Policies of Genocide. Jews and Soviet Prisoners of War in Nazi Germany* (London – Boston – Sydney: Allen & Unwin, 1986).

Hitler, Adolf, *Mein Kampf* (München: Zentralverlag der NSDAP. Frz. Eher Nachf., 1935).

Höhne, Heinz, *Der Orden unter dem Totenkopf. Die Geschichte der SS* (München: Gondrom Verlag, 1990).

Im Feuer Vergangen. Tagebücher aus dem Ghetto (Berlin: Verlag Rütten & Loening, 1960).

Im Warschauer Getto. Das Tagebuch des Adam Czerniaków 1939–1942 (München: Verlag C.H. Beck, 1986).

Jäckel, Eberhard and Jürgen Rohwer, eds., *Der Mord an den Juden im Zweiten Weltkrieg. Entschlussbildung und Verwirklichung* (Stuttgart: Deutsche Verlags-Anstalt, 1985).

Jäger, Herbert, *Verbrechen unter totalitärer Herrschaft. Studien zur nationalsozialistischen Gewaltkriminalität* (Frankfurt am Main: Suhrkamp Taschenbuch, 1982).

Jochmann, Werner, *Gesellschaftskrise und Judenfeindschaft in Deutschland 1870–1945* (Hamburg: Hans Christians Verlag, 1988).

Junge, Traudl, *Bis zur letzten Stunde. Hitlers Sekretärin erzählt ihr Leben* (München: List Taschenbuch, 2002).

Kater, Michael H., *The Nazi Party. A Social Profile of Members and Leaders, 1919–1945* (Cambridge: Harvard University Press, 1983).

Kater, Michael H., *Doctors under Hitler* (Chapel Hill and London: The University of North Carlina Press, 1989).

Katsh, Abraham I., ed., *Scroll of Agony. The Warsaw Diary of Chaim I. Kaplan* (London: Hamish Hamilton, 1966).

Kelman, Herbert C. and V. Lee Hamilton, *Crimes of Obedience. Toward a Social Psychology of Authority and Responsibility* (New Haven and London: Yale University Press, 1989).

Kempner, Robert M.W., *Ankläger einer Epoche. Lebenserinnerungen* (Frankfurt am Main: Ullstein Verlag, 1986).

Kermish, Joseph, ed., *To Live with Honor and Die with Honor. Selected Documents from the Warsaw Ghetto Underground Archives "O.S." (Oneg Shabbath)* (Jerusalem: Yad Vashem, 1986).

Klee, Ernst, *"Euthanasie im NS-Staat." Die "Vernichtung lebensunwerten Lebens"* (Frankfurt am Main: S. Fischer Verlag, 1983).

Klee, Ernst, *Was sie taten – was sie wurden. Ärzte, Juristen und andere Beteiligte am Kranken- oder Judenmord* (Frankfurt am Main: Fischer Taschenbuch Verlag, 1986).

Klee, Ernst, ed., *Dokumente zur "Euthanasie"* (Frankfurt am Main: Fischer Taschenbuch Verlag, 1986).

Klee, Ernst and Willi Dressen. eds., *"Gott mit uns". Der deutsche Vernichtungskrieg im Osten 1939–1945* (Frankfurt am Main: S. Fischer Verlag, 1989).

Klee, Ernst and Willi Dressen. eds., *"Die SA Jesu Christi". Die Kirche im Banne Hitlers* (Frankfurt am Main: Fischer Taschenbuch Verlag, 1989).

Klee, Ernst and Willi Dressen. eds., *Das Personenlexikon zum Dritten Reich. Wer war was vor und nach 1945* (Frankfurt am Main: S. Fischer Verlag, 2003).

Klee, Ernst and Willi Dressen. eds., *Auschwitz. Täter, Gehilfen, Opfer und was aus ihnen wurde. Ein Personenlexikon* (Frankfurt am Main: S. Fischer Verlag, 2013).

Klee, Ernst, Willi Dressen and Volker Riess, eds., *"Schöne Zeiten". Judenmord aus der Sicht der Täter und Gaffer* (Frankfurt am Main: S. Fischer Verlag, 1988).

Klemperer, Victor, *LTI. Notizbuch eines Philologen* (Leipzig: Reclam Verlag, 1975).

Klemperer, Victor, *Ich will Zeugnis ablegen bis zum letzten. Tagebücher 1933–1945*. 2 vols, (Berlin: Aufbau-Verlag, 1996).

Klepper, Jochen, *Unter dem Schatten Deiner Flügel. Aus den Tagebüchern der Jahre 1932–1942* (Stuttgart: Deutsche Verlags-Anstalt, 1956).

Koestler, Arthur, *Bricks to Babel. A Selection from 50 Years of his Writings, Chosen and with New Commentary by the Author* (New York: Random House, 1980).

Koestler, Arthur, *The Yogi and the Commissar and Other Essays* (London: Hutchinson & Co., 1983).

Kogon, Eugen, *Der SS-Staat* (Stockholm: Bermann-Fischer Verlag, 1947).

Kogon, Eugen, Hermann Langbein, Adalbert Rückerl, eds., *Nationalsozialistische Massentötungen durch Giftgas. Eine Dokumentation* (Frankfurt am Main: S. Fischer Verlag, 1983).

Krause, Peter, *Der Eichmann-Prozess in der deutschen Presse* (Frankfurt am Main: Campus Verlag, 2002).

Krummacher, Friedrich A., ed., *Die Kontroverse. Hannah Arendt, Eichmann und die Juden* (München: Nymphenburger Verlagshandlung, 1964).

Kühne, Thomas, *Belonging and Genocide. Hitler's Community, 1918–1945* (New Haven and London: Yale University Press, 2010).

Kulka, Otto D. und Eberhard Jäckel, eds., *Die Juden in den geheimen NS-Stimmungsberichten 1933–1945* (Düsseldorf: Droste Verlag, 2004).

Lamm, Hans, ed., *Der Eichmann-Prozess in der deutschen öffentlichen Meinung* (Frankfurt am Main: Ner-Tamid-Verlag, 1961).

Lang, Jochen von, ed., *Das Eichmann-Protokoll. Tonbandaufzeichnungen der israelischen Verhöre* (Frankfurt am Main – Berlin – Vienna: Ullstein Buch, 1985).

Langbein, Hermann, ed., *Im Namen des deutschen Volkes. Zwischenbilanz der Prozesse wegen nationalsozialistischer Verbrechen* (Wien: Europa Verlag, 1963).

Langbein, Hermann, ed., *... wir haben es getan. Selbstporträts in Tagebüchern und Briefen 1939–1945* (Wien: Europa Verlag, 1964).

Langbein, Hermann, ed., *Menschen in Auschwitz* (Wien: Europa Verlag, 1987).

Laqueur, Walter, *The Terrible Secret. Suppression of the Truth about Hitler's "Final Solution"* (Harmondsworth: Penguin Books, 1982).

Less, Avner W., ed., *Der Staat Israel gegen Adolf Eichmann* (Weinheim: Beltz Athenäum Verlag, 1995).

Lewin, Abraham, *A Cup of Tears. A Diary of the Warsaw Ghetto* in A. Polonsky ed., Oxford: Basil Blackwell, 1988).

Lewy, Guenther, ' "Mit festem Schritt ins neue Reich." Die katholische Kirche zwischen Kreuz und Hakenkreuz', *Der Spiegel* 1965/15, 85–105.

Lewy, Guenter, *Perpetrators. The World of the Holocaust Killers* (Oxford: Oxford University Press, 2017).

Lichtenstein, Heiner, *Im Namen des Volkes? Eine persönliche Bilanz der NS-Prozesse* (Köln: Bund-Verlag, 1984).

Loewy, Hanno and Andrzej Bodek, eds., *'Les Vrais Riches'- Notizen am Rand. Ein Tagebuch aus dem Ghetto Lodz (Mai bis August 1944)* (Leipzig: Reclam Verlag, 1997).

Lozowick, Yaacov, *Hitler's Bureaucrats. The Nazi Security Police and the Banality of Evil* (London and New York: Continuum, 2002).

Lustiger, Arno, ed., *The Black Book of Polish Jewry. An Account of the Martyrdom of Polish Jewry under the Nazi Occupation* (Bodenheim:

Syndikat Buchgesellschaft, 1995; photostatic reprint; originally published New York 1943).

Luyendijk, Joris, *Swimming with Sharks. Inside the World of the Bankers* (London: Guardian Books and Faber & Faber, 2016).

Marrus, Michael R., *The Holocaust in History* (Toronto: Lester & Orpen Dennys, 1987).

Maser, Werner, *Adolf Hitler: Mein Kampf. Geschichte, Auszüge, Kommentare* (München: Moewig, 1983).

Matthias, Erich and Rudolf Morsey, eds., *Das Ende der Parteien 1933. Darstellungen und Dokumente* (Düsseldorf: Athenäum/Droste Taschenbücher, 1979).

Mayer, Milton, *They thought they were free. The Germans 1933–1945* (Chicago and London: The University of Chicago Press, 1967).

Mildt, Dick de, *In the Name of the People. Perpetrators of Genocide in the Reflection of their Post-War Prosecution in West-Germany. The 'Euthanasia' and 'Aktion Reinhard' Trial Cases* (The Hague – London – Boston: Martinus Nijhoff Publishers, 1996).

Milgram, Stanley, *Obedience to Authority. An Experimental View* (New York: HarperPerennial, 1975).

Mitscherlich, Alexander and Fred Mielke, eds., *Medizin ohne Menschlichkeit. Dokumente des Nürnberger Ärzteprozesses* (Frankfurt am Main: Fischer Taschenbuch Verlag, 2012).

Mitscherlich, Alexander, Fred Mielke, and Margarete Mitscherlich, eds., *Die Unfähigkeit zu Trauern. Grundlagen kollektiven Verhaltens* (München: R. Piper & Co. Verlag, 1967).

Moritz, Klaus and Ernst Noam, eds., *Justiz und Judenverfolgung Band 2. NS-Verbrechen vor Gericht 1945–1955. Dokumente aus hessischen Justizakten* (Wiesbaden: Kommission für die Geschichte der Juden in Hessen, 1978).

Mosse, Werner E., ed., *Entscheidungsjahr 1932. Zur Judenfrage in der Endphase der Weimarer Republik. Ein Sammelband* (Tübingen: J.C.B. Mohr, 1965).

Mulisch, Harry, *De zaak 40/61. Een reportage* (Amsterdam: Uitgeverij de Bezige Bij, 1964; first published 1961).

Müller, Ingo, *Furchtbare Juristen. Die unbewältigte Vergangenheit unserer Justiz* (München: Kindler Verlag, 1987).

Müller-Hill, Benno, *Tödliche Wissenschaft. Die Aussonderung von Juden, Zigeunern und Geisteskranken 1933–1945* (Reinbek bei Hamburg: Rowohlt, 1984).

Nach dem Eichmann Prozess. Zu einer Kontroverse über die Haltung der Juden (Tel Aviv: Bitaon Publishing Co., 1963).

Nellesen, Bernd, ed., *Der Prozess von Jerusalem: Ein Dokument* (Düsseldorf and Wien: Econ, 1964).

Newman, Leonard S. and Ralph Erber, eds., *Understanding Genocide. The Social Psychology of the Holocaust* (New York: Oxford University Press, 2002).

Noam, Ernst and Wolf-Arno Kropat, eds., *Justiz und Judenverfolgung Band 1. Juden vor Gericht 1933–1945. Dokumente aus hessischen Justizakten* (Wiesbaden: Kommission für die Geschichte der Juden in Hessen, 1986.

Parliamentary Commission on Banking Standards – Fifth Report – Changing Banking for Good, 12 June 2014. Parliamentary Commission on Banking Standards (www.parliament.uk/bankingstandards).

Pätzold, Kurt and Erika Schwarz, *'Auschwitz war für mich nur ein Bahnhof'. Franz Novak – Der Transportoffizier Adolf Eichmanns* (Berlin: Metropol Verlag, 1994).

Pendorf, Robert, *Mörder und Ermordete. Eichmann und die Judenpolitik des Dritten Reiches* (Hamburg: Rutten & Loening Verlag, 1961).

Peukert, Detlev J. K., *Inside Nazi Germany. Conformity, Opposition and Racism in Everyday Life* (Harmondsworth: Penguin Books, 1989).

Picker, Henry, *Hitlers Tischgespräche im Führerhauptquartier* (Wiesbaden: VMA-Verlag, 1989).

Poliakov, Léon and Josef Wulf, eds., *Das Dritte Reich und die Juden. Dokumente und Berichte* (Wiesbaden: Fourier Verlag, 1989).

Poliakov, Léon and Josef Wulf, ed., *Das Dritte Reich und seine Diener. Auswärtiges Amt, Justiz und Wehrmacht. Dokumente und Berichte* (Wiesbaden: Fourier Verlag, 1989).

Poliakov, Léon and Josef Wulf, ed., *Das Dritte Reich und seine Denker. Dokumente und Berichte* (Wiesbaden: Fourier Verlag, 1989).

Reuth, Ralf Georg, ed., *Joseph Goebbels Tagebücher 1924–1945* 5 vols, (München: Piper Verlag, 2008).

Reynolds, Quentin J., Ephraim Katz and Zwi Aldouby, *Minister of Death: The Adolf Eichmann Story* (New York: Viking Press, 1960).

Ritz, Christian, *Schreibtischtäter vor Gericht. Das Verfahren vor dem Münchner Landgericht wegen der Deportation der niederländischen Juden (1959–1967)* (Paderborn: Ferdinand Schöningh, 2012).

Roazen, Paul, *Freud and his followers* (Harmondsworth: Penguin, 1973).

Rosenbaum, Ron, *Explaining Hitler. The Search for the Origins of his Evil* (New York: Harper Perennial, 1999).

Rosenfeld, Oskar, *Wozu noch Welt. Aufzeichnungen aus dem Getto Lodz.* in H. Loewy ed., (Frankfurt am Main: Verlag Neue Kritik, 1994).

Rothfels, Hans, 'Augenzeugenbericht zu den Massenvergasungen' *Vierteljahreshefte für Zeitgeschichte.* 1953/1, 177–194.

Rückerl, Adalbert, ed., *NS-Prozesse. Nach 25 Jahren Strafverfolgung: Möglichkeiten – Grenzen – Ergebnisse* (Karlsruhe: C.F. Müller Juristischer Verlag, 1971).

Rückerl, Adalbert, ed., *NS-Vernichtungslager im Spiegel deutscher Strafprozesse. Belzec, Sobibor, Treblinka, Chelmno* (München: Deutscher Taschenbuch Verlag, 1977).

Rückerl, Adalbert, *NS-Verbrechen vor Gericht. Versuch einer Vergangenheitsbewältigung* (Heidelberg: C.F. Müller Juristischer Verlag, 1984).

Scheffler, Wolfgang, 'Chelmno, Sobibor, Belzec und Majdanek', in E. Jäckel and J. Rohwer, eds., *Der Mord an den Juden im Zweiten Weltkrieg* (Stuttgart: Deutsche Verlags-Anstalt, 1985), 145–156.

Schelvis, Jules, *Vernietigingskamp Sobibor* (Amsterdam: De Bataafsche Leeuw, 1997).

Schmidt, Matthias, *Albert Speer: Das Ende eines Mythos. Aufdeckung einer Geschichtsverfälschung* (Bern and München: Wilhelm Goldmann Verlag, 1982).

Schmorak, Dov B., *Der Prozess Eichmann* (Wien: Hans Deutsch Verlag, 1964).

Schmuhl, Hans-Walter, *Rassenhygiene, Nationalsozialismus, Euthanasie. Von der Verhütung zur Vernichtung 'lebensunwerten Lebens', 1890–1945* (Göttingen: Vandenhoeck & Ruprecht, 1992).

Schoenbaum, David, *Hitler's Social Revolution. Class and Status in Nazi Germany 1933–1939* (New York and London: W.W. Norton & Company, 1980).

Schroers, Rolf, 'Der banale Eichmann und seine Opfer' in F. A. Krummacher, ed., *Die Kontroverse. Hannah Arendt, Eichmann und die Juden* (München: Nymphenburger Verlagshandlung, 1964).

Sereny, Gitta, *Into that Darkness. An Examination of Conscience* (London: Pan Books, 1977).

Sereny, Gitta, *Am Abgrund: Gespräche mit dem Henker* (München and Zürich: Piper Verlag, 1995).

Sereny, Gitta, *Albert Speer. His Battle with Truth* (London: Picador, 1996).

Sloan, Jacob, ed., *Notes from the Warsaw Ghetto. The Journal of Emmanuel Ringelblum* (New York: ibooks, inc., 2006).

Speer, Albert, *Erinnerungen* (Frankfurt am Main – Berlin – Wien: Ullstein Verlag, 1982).

Staff, Ilse, ed., *Justiz im Dritten Reich. Eine Dokumentation* (Frankfurt am Main: Fischer Bücherei, 1964).

Stangneth, Bettina, *Eichmann vor Jerusalem. Das unbehelligte Leben eines Massenmörders* (Zürich and Hamburg: Arche Literaur Verlag, 2011).

Staub, Ervin, *The Roots of Evil. The Origins of Genocide and Other Group Violence* (Cambridge: Cambridge University Press, 1989).

Swaan, Abram de, *Compartimenten van vernietiging. Over genocidale regimes en hun daders* (Amsterdam: Prometheus – Bert Bakker, 2014).

Swaan, Abram de, *The Killing Compartments. The Mentality of Mass Murder* (New Haven and London: Yale University Press, 2015).

Trunk, Isaiah, *Judenrat. The Jewish Councils in Eastern Europe under Nazi Occupation* (Lincoln: University of Nebraska Press, 1996).

Tuturow, Norman E., ed., *War Crimes, War Criminals, and War Crimes Trials. An Annotated Bibliography and Source Book* (New York – Westport – Connecticut – London: Greenwood Press, 1986).

Wegner, Bernd, *Hitlers politische Soldaten: die Waffen-SS 1933–1945* (Paderborn: Ferdinand Schöningh, 1983).

Wehler, Hans-Ulrich, *Deutsche Gesellschaftsgeschichte 1914–1949* (Bonn: Bundeszentrale für politische Bildung, 2009).

Weissenborn, Günther, ed., *Der Lautlose Aufstand. Bericht über die Widerstandsbewegung des deutschen Volkes. 1933–1945* (Hamburg: Rowohlt, 1962).

Welzer, Harald, *Täter. Wie aus ganz normalen Menschen Massenmörder werden* (Frankfurt am Main: Fischer Tascehnbuch Verlag, 2011).

Wiesenthal, Simon, *Moordenaars onder ons* (Amsterdam and Brussels: Elsevier, 1968).

Wistrich, Robert, *Wer war Wer im Dritten Reich. Ein biographisches Lexikon* (Frankfurt am Main: Fischer Taschenbuch Verlag, 1987).

Wulf, Joseph, *Das Dritte Reich und seine Vollstrecker. Die Liquidation der Juden im Warschauer Ghetto. Dokumente und Berichte* (Wiesbaden: Fourier Verlag, 1989).

Yad, Vashem, ed., *Blackbook of Localities whose Jewish Population was Exterminated by the Nazis* (Jerusalem: Weiss Press, 1965).

Zuccotti, Susan, *The Italians and the Holocaust. Persecution, Rescue & Survival* (London: Peter Halban, 1987).

Zweig, Stefan, *Die Welt von Gestern. Erinnerungen eines Europäers* (Frankfurt am Main: Fischer Taschenbuch Verlag, 2013).

Newspaper articles

Abend-Zeitung, München 28 January 1967: 'Immer nur Richtlinien'.

Allgemeine Zeitung, Mainz 30 May 1970: 'Schwiegersohn lieferte KZ-Stangl aus'.

Die Welt, 17 November 1964: 'Rudel schoss Akten in Brand'.

Die Welt, 25 August 1965: 'Hauptangeklagter Franz fordert Freispruch'.

Die Welt, 11 March 1988: 'Als es um das Kreuz ging, rebellierten die Oldenburger'.

Die Zeit, Nr.31, 30 July 1982: 'Die angebliche Entlarvung. Albert Speers wiederholt nur Allzubekanntes'.

Essener Tageblatt, 13 December 1966: 'Das letzte Wort der elf von Sobibor: "Sie werden keinen grausamen Zug in meinem Gesicht finden können"'.

Frankfurter Allgemeine Zeitung, 17 November 1964: 'Treueprämien für Euthanasie-Angestellte'.

Leverkusener Anzeiger /Kölner Stadt-Anzeiger, 10 June 1970: 'Was die Zeugin Stangl vor Gericht aussagte'.

Main Post, 8 June 2007: 'Aus Holland in den Tod'.

Münchner Merkur, 18 February 1967: 'Harster und Zoepf wiederholen ihr Schuldbekenntnis'.

Neue Rhein Zeitung, 20 October 1964: 'Zuhörer protestieren laut'.

Rheinische Post, 14 October 1964: 'Alle beschuldigen Franz'.

Rheinische Post, 16 December 1970.

Rheinische Post, 5 February 1965: 'Zeig dich mit deinem Hund...'.

Ruhr-Nachrichten, 13 April 1966: 'Sobibor ... was ist das?'.

Ruhr-Nachrichten, 13 December 1966: ' "Sie werden keinen grausamen Zug in meinem Gesicht finden können"'.

Stern, 9 July 1967: 'Mord hinter dem Guckloch'.

Stern, 22 March 1984: 'Der Mörder und sein Zeuge'.

Westdeutsche Allgemeine, 9 October 1964: 'Peitschenhiebe bis zum Massengrab'.

Westfalenpost, 17 November 1964: ' "T4"-Stiftung schickte Wachmännern Rotwein'.

Index on persons

A
Adenauer, Konrad 48, 74
Alexander, Leo 134
Allers, Dietrich 34, 35, 38, 39, 123, 134, 135, 139
Arendt, Hannah 17, 30, 31, 90, 100–109
Arnoni, M.S. 7, 11
Asche, Kurt 96, 128
Aschenauer, Rudolf 27–29

B
Bach-Zelewski, Erich von dem 21, 22, 26, 74, 133, 134
Bauer, Erich 54, 116, 119
Becker, Hans-Joachim 35, 123
Best, Werner 77, 96
Bettelheim, Bruno 10
Blankenburg, Werner 34, 38, 76
Blau 81
Bohne, Gerhard 135
Bosshammer, Friedrich 95, 126
Bouhler, Philipp 41, 43, 44, 46
Brack, Viktor 34, 35, 36, 38, 39, 45
Brandt, Karl 41
Braune, Gerhard 42, 47
Browning, Christopher 98, 131
Bullock, Alan 113

C
Cohen, Elie Aron 21, 22

D
Dawidowicz, Lucy 22, 28
Dollfuss, Engelbert 61, 65

E
Eberl, Irmfried 70
Eichmann, Adolf 20, 24, 29–31, 51, 53, 67, 94, 96, 99, 100–110, 132, 143, 144
Eigruber, August 62, 139

F
Franz, Kurt 49, 54, 78, 80, 84, 118
Frenzel, Karl 38, 39, 47, 119, 129
Freud, Sigmund 87–89
Fromm, Erich 88

G
Galen, Clemens August Grafvon 47
Ganzenmüller, Albert 94
Globke, Hans 74
Globocnik, Odilo 60, 70, 78, 102
Goldhagen, Daniel 22, 28
Gürtner, Franz 41–46, 48

H
Hagen, Herbert 95, 128
Hahn, Fritz-Gebhardt von 94, 123
Hanke, Karl 93
Harster, Wilhelm 96, 97, 119
Hartmann, Richard 94, 95, 124
Hausner, Gideon 105
Hegener, Richard von 36, 130
Heinrichsohn, Ernst 95, 128
Hering, Gottlieb 69

Heyde, Werner 45
Heydrich, Reinhard 24, 25, 29
Himmler, Heinrich 21, 24, 29,
  52, 70, 90, 93, 105, 138
Hirschfeld, Max 66, 67
Horn, Otto 75, 76, 118
Höss, Rudolf 20, 132, 134
Höttl, Wilhelm 132
Huber, Franz Josef 25, 66
Hueber, Franz 62

I
Ittner, Alfred 36, 119

J
Jäger, Herbert 99

K
Kant, Immanuel 30, 105
Kaplan, Chaim 17, 101
Knochen, Helmut 95
Koestler, Arthur 15, 18, 19, 100,
  101, 112
Korff, Modest Alfred Leonhard
  Graf von 96, 130
Kremer, Johann Paul 52, 117
Kreyssig, Lothar 41, 42, 44, 49

L
Lambert, Erwin 50, 92,
  118, 119
Lammers, Hans 42, 43
Lanzmann, Claude 131
Laqueur, Walter 104
Less, Avner 101, 106, 107, 109
Lewin, Abraham 19
Linden, Herbert 35
Lischka, Kurt 95, 128
Lorent, Friedrich 35, 36, 123
Lorenz, Konrad 54, 55

Lubbe, Marinus van der 19
Luyendijk, Joris 91

M
Markut, Herrmann 63
Marrus, Michael 20, 23, 24, 33,
  40, 110
Matthes, Heinrich 49, 50, 118
Maurach, Reinhart 27
Mengele, Josef 99
Mentz, Willi 37–39, 50, 83,
  84, 118
Miete, August 37–39, 50, 118
Morgenstern, Christian 108
Mulisch, Harry 30, 53
Müller, Heinrich 24, 25, 29, 66
Münzberger, Gustav 50, 118
Musmanno, Michael A. 28

N
Nietzsche, Friedrich 41, 57, 111
Nohel, Vinzenz 142

P
Palmström 108–110
Péguy, Charles 90
Prohaska, Georg 63–65, 68, 69

R
Rademacher, Franz 94, 121
Reichleitner, Franz 68, 139
Reinhard, Hellmuth 94, 124
Rückerl, Adalbert 55, 57
Rum, Franz 36, 50, 118
Rüter, C.F. 10

S
Scheffler, Wolfgang 36, 38
Schiller, Friedrich 15
Schirach, Baldur von 142

Schirach, Henriette von 142
Schlegelberger, Franz 43–45
Schmiedel, Fritz 36
Schneider, Carl 45, 46
Schneider, Willy 36
Schuschnigg, Kurt 65
Schweitzer, Albert 53
Sereny, Gitta 57, 58, 61, 62, 64, 68, 69, 78–81, 84, 85, 92, 93
Servatius, Robert 105, 106
Siebert, Gerhardt 35
Sitwell, Osbert 18, 19
Speer, Albert 92, 93, 97, 142
Stadie, Otto 49, 118
Stangl, Franz 36, 47, 57–85, 106, 125, 139
Stangneth, Bettina 87, 100, 101, 107
Steiner, George 87
Suchomel, Franz 36, 50, 75, 118
Swaan, Abram de 102–104, 109

V
Vorberg, Reinhold 35, 39, 123

W
Wagner, Franz 36
Werner, Ludwig 63–65
Werner, Paul 68
Wiesenthal, Simon 53, 59
Wille, Bruno 63
Wirth, Christian 39, 40, 47, 52, 60, 70, 73–77
Wisliceny, Dieter 20, 100, 123
Wöhrn, Fritz 95, 125
Wolf, Franz 36, 119
Wolf, Josef 36, 135
Wolff, Karl 93, 94, 117
Wolkers, Jan 111, 113

Z
Zoepf, Willelm 96, 97, 119
Zweig Stefan 65